video for development

A Casebook from Vietnam

Su Braden with Than Thi Thien Huong

Oxfam UK and Ireland

facing page Villagers in Minh Quy viewing one of their tapes.

Published by Oxfam UK and Ireland
First published 1998

© Oxfam UK and Ireland 1998

A catalogue record for this publication is available from the British Library.

ISBN 0 85598 370 1

Published by Oxfam UK and Ireland, 274 Banbury Road, Oxford OX2 7DZ, UK
(registered as a charity, no. 202918)

Available in Ireland from Oxfam in Ireland, 19 Clanwilliam Terrace, Dublin 2 (tel. 01 661 8544). Addresses of agents and distributors are given on the last page.

Designed by Oxfam Design Department OX117/RB/97
Printed by Oxfam Print Unit

Oxfam UK and Ireland is a member of Oxfam International.

cover photograph: Su Braden

Su Braden

Contents

Acknowledgements v

Introduction 1

■ 1 The role of video in participatory development 13

■ 2 Participant observation in Ky Nam 27

■ 3 Participatory research and analysis in Ky Nam 41

■ 4 Conflict: the private and the public 51

■ 5 Re-presentation and advocacy 59

■ 6 Typhoons and evaluations 69

■ 7 Lessons learned — and the way forward 87

Notes 101

Sources and further reading 104

Oxfam/Keith Bernstein

above Ky Anh District.

Acknowledgements

My thanks to Michael Etherton, who was the Representative of Oxfam UK and Ireland in Hanoi at the time, for his imaginative and courageous idea of setting up the Video Pilot Project in Vietnam. Thanks too, for their help and encouragement with the writing of this case-study, to Heather Grady, the current Country Representative, and to Susi Arnott and Tony Dowmunt for their help and comments here in the UK. Thanks to Haida Paul for all her useful thoughts, as well as to I.V. Domingo and our colleagues from Laos who all worked with such commitment and did so much to make our time in Ky Nam a valuable and enjoyable experience. Above all, thanks to Oxfam colleagues Than Thi Thien Huong, who contributed to this book with so many e-mails, reports, and wonderful discussions; and to Nguyen Minh Cuong and Do Thanh Binh. Their insights, dedication, and hard work taught me much. They have continued to develop the uses of participatory video in Vietnam with great success. Finally, I must thank Catherine Robinson, my editor at Oxfam Publications, for all her hard work and patience.

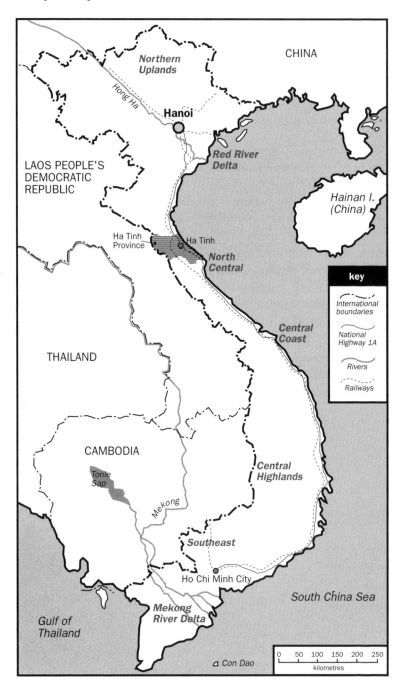

above Map of Vietnam, featuring Ha Tinh Province.

Introduction

In July 1995, a small group of community communication and development workers took part in a pilot project to explore the potential of participatory video with villagers in a commune in the North-Central region of Vietnam. They set out to test a proposition that poor communities '... *particularly poor women, who must take decisions about changes in their society which will affect their workloads, access to markets, the health of themselves and their families, and the education of their children, need to "practise" representing themselves to others. They need to practise articulating their own resources and their own choices.'* [1]

The team included three Vietnamese staff from the Hanoi office of Oxfam UK and Ireland (referred to from now on as 'Oxfam'), a group of communication workers and women's organisers from Laos, a representative from World Neighbors in Indonesia, and a Canadian film editor. They spent three days preparing and practising their participatory video skills in Oxfam's office in Hanoi and then travelled south to a small commune, Ky Nam, where they spent ten days working with villagers. What follows is an account of the work that took place, and the views of the villagers about this work, recorded one year later.

Each context is unique and presents its own peculiar sets of problems. The reason for writing this book is to document and offer insights into the use of video in participatory community-building, in relation to the specific context of rural Vietnam. We hope that this case-study may be useful in broadening the debates about participation and representation as they relate to this and other contexts. And that by offering this account, warts and all, we will encourage those for whom 'best practice' in participatory development is always a goal — but probably a mirage.

My own role in the pilot project was to act as a trainer in the use of participatory video. The account of the training and field processes which follows is presented from my point of view as a trainer, with the benefit of retrospective research by and dialogue with Than Thi Thien Huong, Oxfam's Programme Officer for Advocacy and Communication in Vietnam, who took part in the project as a trainee.

Ky Nam

Ky Nam, in the district of Ky Anh, in the south of Ha Tinh Province, is the last commune on what was the border of the old North: situated on the coastal plain, it nestles against the mountains which divide the North and the South. Up above the commune, a stone arch and a shrine on the Ngang Pass mark the traditional crossing point of armies from the older kingdoms of Viet and Nam, en route for battle against each other, or against the Chinese. Soldiers pausing there on their way to fight may have burnt incense at the shrine, or scratched a verse or a message on the inner walls of the arch. In the twentieth century the same Pass was used by fighters against the French, and 25 years ago soldiers recorded their thoughts in the same way, as they moved south to resist the US military. Ironically, only a few such messages are visible today, because the interior of the arch, perhaps with tourism in mind, has been cleaned up. Yet the memories of those wars, and especially the American War (1955–1975), are not far beneath the surface of the minds of local people, and the earth that they till. The war left its inheritance too in genetic deformities caused by the defoliant

below A Ky Nam villager demonstrating a war-time lantern, designed to avoid detection by US bombers overhead.

Oxfam/Sean Sprague

chemical Agent Orange. Left-over ordnance can still blow off the arm of a young boy chopping a tree for fire-wood in the early morning, as we were to witness.

The Vietnamese have buried their war dead, if not the after-effects of war. Their Missing in Action teams have long dispersed, but in July 1995 the Americans were still looking for their airmen, missing in action on the hillsides above Ky Nam. The villagers, employed by the American MIA team to dig up the remains of a B52 bomber, said they had been told by Commune leaders that the remaining trade embargoes imposed by the Western world would be lifted only when it was made known to the US government that they had co-operated in the search. The villagers' desperate need for the daily rate paid by these Americans, camped at the river mouth, offers a graphic illustration of how the peace is being won under the new economic world order.

In other ways, too, the history of Ky Nam reflects its particular social character. It was, in the times of Vietnam's royal past, a penal colony for political dissidents, and the people of the commune are proud of their heritage as independent thinkers — while suspecting that their poverty and the neglect of their far-flung commune may be the result of this reputation.

> *We have historical monuments that our ancestors left for generations.*
> *The King's temple is painted to make it more beautiful.*
> *We burn incense so the God up there knows,*
> *and our people have a better life and peace everywhere.*
> *We should give gratitude to those who fought for peace.*
> *People should not forget the Revolution's merit.*
> *Every ox and every buffalo that is brought back to us is from our Party.*
> *Let's hope the Revolutionary road will be glorious...*

This song, composed by an old farmer in the Ky Nam Commune village of Minh Duc, reflects something of the proud and diverse inheritance of the area. The ancestors and their royal connections, recalled in the smoke of incense, are celebrated as part of the same world as the Revolution, and commemorated along with the horrors and sorrows of war.

Geography and climate

Ky Nam is one of 31 communes in Ky Anh District, in the North-Central District of Vietnam, each composed of a cluster of smaller villages. The district town is the seat of the district administration. In 1993 the District population was calculated at 149,128, of whom more than half lacked adequate rice (see Table 1) for three–six months of the year. The climate is marked by periods of drought, alternating with severe typhoons: 36 between 1962 and 1991, about

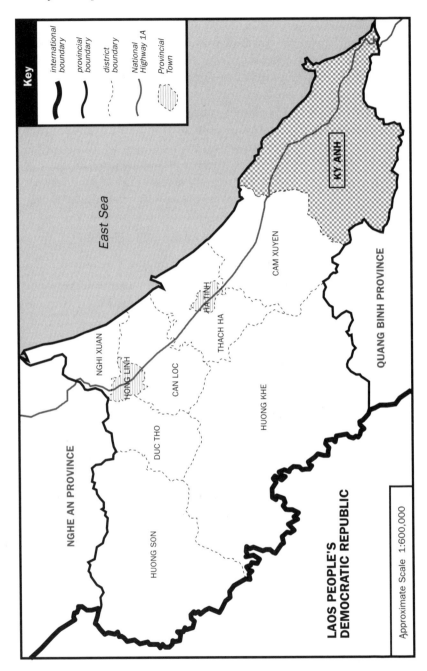

above A map of Ha Tinh Province, showing Ky Anh District.

one every 18 months, of which nearly half were Level 10 or higher, causing sea-water to flood the villages and rice fields. Between 1987 and 1991, nine typhoons caused 12,375 houses to collapse, and over 7,200 hectares — half the cultivable land in the District — were flooded by sea-water.[2] The Ky Anh coastal plain is criss-crossed by small streams flowing steeply down from the mountains and out into the South China Sea. Their use for irrigation is dependent on hydraulic works, many of which have also been destroyed by typhoons.

Table 1: Population and land

	Viet Nam	**Ky Anh**	**Ky Nam** [a]
Population	70 million — the world's twelfth largest — and growing rapidly. 60% under 21.	149,128 (1993), of whom more than half lack adequate food[b] for 3–6 months of the year.	Approx. 1,719
Disposition	80% live in rural areas.	31 communes; one district town.	420 households, 67 classified by the CPC[c] as 'hungry' (producing no more than 8 kg of rice per head per month), and 243 estimated as 'poor' (under 13 kg per head per month). 310 households targeted by the Commune for the government's Hunger Eradication programme.
Land classification	Following the collapse of the co-operative system in 1986, the State decreed that farmers should be allocated land for private ownership. Under Decree 10, not only agricultural land but also forest and hillsides will be given to individuals.	105,278 hectares, of which only 14,845 (14%) can be cultivated. 50% of this cultivable land was flooded by sea-water between 1987 and 1991.	Land classified as 'one-harvest land',[d] dry land, or irrigated land. So far private land allocation has not been completed by the CPC.

(a) Figures supplied by the Commune People's Committee, July 1995.

(b) 13–15 kg of rice per capita per month.

(c) Commune People's Committee.

(d) This classification will be used by the Commune when allocation of land into private ownership begins.

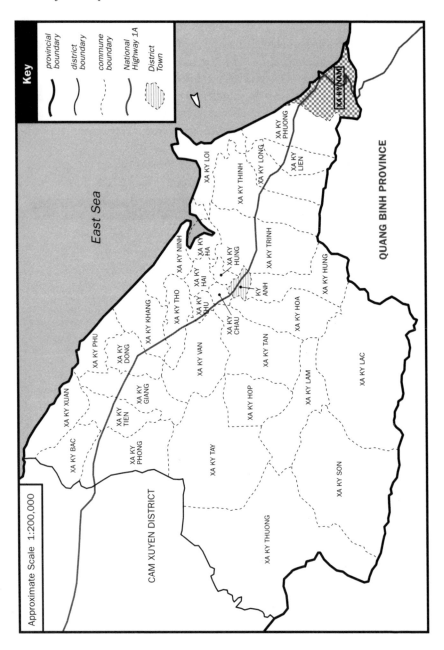

above A map of Ky Anh District, showing Ky Nam Commune.

Poverty

Ky Anh District is set above the 17th parallel, which once marked the division between North and South Vietnam. The political location of Ky Anh, lying across the Ho Chi Minh Trail, led to remorseless bombing during the American war. The district administration was very active against the French and the Americans and is still today deeply committed to the Revolution.

Ky Nam is one of the poorest communes in Ky Anh — but there are no rich people in these villages, only gradations of poverty. In 1992 severe food shortages led Oxfam to truck rice into Ky Anh. During the last six years, in collaboration with the Water Resource University of Hanoi, Oxfam has helped Ky Anh people to construct sea dykes, measuring 33 km, around six of the most vulnerable communes. There is now striking visual evidence of the results, in the form of a vast green and productive area behind the dykes.

Ky Nam itself, farther down the coast, and with a smaller population, was not included in this scheme; its fields stretch out in a large patchwork of brown, parched lands. Ky Nam people may feel that this is just part of their historical heritage. They still have no electricity, no television, and no secondary school.

The main development in the district is taking place along Highway One, which carries all the road traffic between the North and the South of the country and provides market outlets for those with produce to sell. And yet, because of the problems of flooding and drought, the villagers of Ky Nam gain little benefit from this traffic. They have no cultivated produce to bring to the roadside and are forced to sell firewood collected from the forest above the commune. These bundles of wood are sold on at a considerable profit by passing truck drivers when they reach the southern side of the mountain. Oxfam staff once asked a representative of the District Authority why officials did not stop Ky Nam people stripping the growth from the forest to sell as firewood. After all, it was the authorities who had placed a prominent sign at the point where Highway One crosses the commune, declaring 'Our Forest is Our Future'. The official replied: 'The people must eat.'

Vietnam: the economic context

Since unification in 1975, Vietnam has been dealt a poor hand in developing a stable economy. The US-led trade embargo eliminated trade not only with the USA, but also with her allies, and blocked virtually all Western economic assistance. This was followed by the faltering of the Eastern European economies during the break-up of the Soviet bloc. In 1989, inflation in Vietnam reached 700 per cent, causing massive unemployment and under-employment, and leading the government to respond to threats of social unrest by adopting a policy of renovation (*doi moi*): the creation of a socialist market economy. Restrictions on private enterprise were eased; liberal policies on foreign investment were implemented; price controls were reduced; land-use rights were reformed; and a new monetary policy was adopted.

As a result of *doi moi*, Vietnam became one of the world's top rice producers; inflation was reduced to a single digit; and GDP began an upward curve. In the USA, commercial and other interests began a campaign to remove the embargo; the campaign bore fruit when the Clinton administration lifted most of the restrictions in February 1994. The down-side of the new influx of capital and goods that resulted from the combination of *doi moi* and the lifting of the US trade embargo was the lack of local infrastructural support for local industry. Imported goods flooded the consumer market, but Vietnamese consumers were buying more than they produced.

Cultural change

Perhaps none of the almost constant and violent changes that have beset Vietnam over the centuries will prove to have had a more profound effect than the enormous political and economic changes that are currently taking place. They represent a cultural revolution that must influence the ways in which Vietnamese people live and think. It is a revolution that appears to have arrived almost by stealth. Of course, it has concrete and physical manifestations: new buildings in the cities, more vehicles, new roads, Rupert Murdoch's Star TV satellite service from Hong Kong, a boom in the advertising industry, more imported consumables, more foreign business, and more tourism; but they also bring a host of new and less tangible political and cultural influences. These influences can be understood most clearly through observation of the Vietnamese communications media.

Vietnamese intellectuals and the media, specifically newspapers, did much to mobilise the oppressed population to support the Nationalist cause throughout the 1930s and 1940s. Similarly, throughout the American War, the Hanoi government in the north and the National Liberation Front in the south operated clandestine radio stations above and below ground.[3] Through-out the 1970s, radio and TV networks were tightly controlled by the Party, although opposition continued to be voiced (some by those opposed to Communism) via illegal radio stations. In the south, 'video cafes' showed a range of material brought in from elsewhere.

The latest economic changes have also brought changes in the control of the mass media.[4] Today, the Ministry of Culture operates two broadcasting networks, Radio Voice of Vietnam and Vietnam Television. Sixty per cent of

Oxfam/Ben Fawcett

above A roadside market in Ky Anh District.

the population are able to receive Radio Vietnam, but, according to Hiebert (1995),[5] a recent survey by Ogilvy and Mather in Ho Chi Minh City found that only about 17 per cent regularly listened to the radio, while 71 per cent claimed to watch television.

Vietnam Television offers three channels of programming to a network of provincial and district stations, one of which is in Ky Anh, available to about 45 per cent of the population. The third channel was launched in 1993, with a marked change in programming, signalling a new move by the government; the intention is to appeal to a mass audience in a changed economic climate. The Ministry described the third channel's programmes as offering 'sports, economic news, full-length movies and beauty contests', and hinted at the possible future privatisation of the service. In 1996 the channel introduced the SV 96 Forum — an open forum in which students discussed a range of social/political and cultural issues; this programme was later replaced with another open-debate programme involving government and students — mainly funded by Pepsi-Cola. This new channel, VT-3, brings State television into direct competition with STAR-TV and CNN-Television — some of whose reports are frequently included in the evening newscasts of VTV.

Watching VTV, one is struck by the enormous amount of advertising, including, notably, campaigns to promote Coca-Cola and Nestlé's baby milk formula (both banned from the media in India at one time or another). Coca-

9

Cola alone was reported to have spent US$250,000 in the first ten days following the lifting of the trade embargo in Vietnam.[6]

Cultural and political representation

The Vietnam Communist Party has a policy of economic liberalisation within the Communist framework, but is concerned about the control of the social ills, such as prostitution and drug abuse, that often accompany modernisation. The transition to a market economy in Vietnam shows all the signs of pain that have been experienced in other countries where such changes have occurred. In Vietnam, with its strong traditions of intellectual and cultural life and high levels of literacy, cultural domination from outside threatens not only the production of elite culture, but also the use of culture as a form of expression by the mass of the population. 'Entertainment' with a mass appeal, conducive to consumerism, threatens increasingly to overwhelm the traditions of political participation and debate in Vietnamese society.

In the past, learning was revered, and stories of academic success are embedded in traditional story telling. The education system reflected the relationships between local and national government. Primary education was the business of the villages, and secondary education the business of the District or Provinces; students who progressed beyond these ended up at Van Mieu, the University of Hanoi, where a doctorate was awarded by the King, together sometimes with the prize of the hand of a royal princess in marriage. The stories of these processes are told in the traditional scenes of the water puppets, still performed today in Hanoi, and in imagery in the stone courtyards of Van Mieu.

There is no longer an obvious common enemy whose very presence had always created a sense of unity and common purpose, as well as strengthening the heroic cultural heritage of this vulnerable country. The Party has expressed its political concerns about the dangers of the new technologies, and may try to limit access to certain forms of telecommunications technology to certain groups only, for example the international business community. But such concerns appear to touch fewer and fewer Vietnamese, and even Party officials find themselves taking part in the race to consolidate their positions as entrepreneurs and consultants in the chaotically expanding commercial sector.

By stealth, this access to the global village of electronic communication may be eroding a famous Vietnamese tradition of clandestine presses and underground radios, village poetry and songs, that formed the backbone of resistance to the more brutal invasions of Vietnam's past.

Even where there is no electricity, and no TV as yet, poverty itself can become the subject of a new drive for profit. In Ky Nam, Highway One may not

above Ky Anh High School.

bring new markets to the poverty-stricken villagers, but we observed their children being thrown money by a national TV crew seeking to make a sensational documentary about child beggars. A middle-aged father sees his wife off to work and minds the children, while she conducts her 'faded flower' business with the truck drivers. After all, they must eat.

The video project in Ky Nam

It was in this context of change within Vietnamese culture — changes that are affecting everyone economically, socially, and culturally — that Oxfam's pilot project to explore the participatory uses of video took place. It was a tribute to Oxfam's good relations with the District authorities in Ky Anh and the Vietnam Communist Party that the use of video with and by villagers was permitted. But, at the same time, it raised questions about how the villagers who participated would be monitored, and how sensitive the pilot team would need to be to the new socio-political context in which they would be working.

Chapter 1 of this book will outline some of the principal concerns that lay behind the Oxfam initiative in Ky Nam, and some of the principles underlying the uses of participatory video. It will raise questions about 'participation'. This will lead into a discussion of the relationship between participation and representation, and the uses of video as a tool for retrieving and reflecting local information, as well as the potential for local groups to re-present their findings and views to others.

Chapter 2 will examine the ways in which Oxfam's organisational perspectives were redefined, as the focus changed from that of the international NGO, based in the UK and in Hanoi, to the point of view of the villagers and the local context.

Chapter 3 will discuss the ways in which the villagers used video to research and retrieve information about their needs and problems, and the learning process involving the villagers and the visiting team will be discussed.

Chapter 4 examines issues of conflict within the commune, and the role of video in objectifying the issues involved, within the private world of the village and eventually in the wider world of the district authorities.

Chapter 5 will look at how villagers represented their findings in three short video programmes, and how they used these programmes to generate communication both within and beyond the villages.

In Chapter 6 a member of Oxfam's programme staff revisits the village, one year later, to gather the views of the villagers and the local authorities on the outcomes of the project.

In Chapter 7 the issues that arose from the evaluation of the pilot project are reviewed from the wider perspective of training and learning in the field, and the implications for the work of non-government development organisations are discussed.

The role of video in participatory development I

Why should an agency like Oxfam be interested in using video as a tool for social development? Video has the potential to retrieve the experiences and reflect back the voices of under-represented people. It can provide an accessible record of testimony, discussions, and activities. Groups and individual participants can use these audio-visual records to discuss and reorganise their opinions and concerns, and they can re-record and add information. When they are satisfied that they have represented what they want to say and show, they can take their information and re-present it to others. Video tapes can act as a conduit for communication between grass-roots communities and those whom under-represented groups would not normally be able to address.

Unfortunately, the advantages of the participatory uses of video do not automatically resolve all the problems of management, planning, timing, sustainability, training, and facilitation that affect other approaches to participatory learning.

Participation and development

To appreciate the significance of the pilot project in Ky Nam Commune, which was set up to investigate the potential of video as a tool for learning, it may be helpful to consider it in the context of recent and current thinking about participatory development.

In the 1960s and 1970s, debates about the meaning of 'participation' were associated with a growing body of theory about grassroots development. Educationists such as Ivan Illich and Paulo Freire devised radical learning programmes with people living on the margins of society. They introduced new and liberal methods of teaching to encourage poor people to think critically about the reasons for their oppression and exclusion. Freire introduced the notion of learning as a process that could lead to social transformation.[1]

Rather than using pre-printed textbooks in adult literacy classes, Freire encouraged learning groups to develop their own materials, based on the daily reality of their lives. This methodology represented an opposition to traditional approaches to learning, which Freire called 'the banking system of education', and replaced it with a process of dialogue between teachers and learners which Freire called 'critical pedagogy'.

Freire's objections to a 'top-down' mode of learning in which marginalised people are treated as passive recipients of knowledge were reflected in a move among development agencies in the 1970s and 1980s to devise methods of working with poor communities which would actively involve them in identifying and solving their own problems. Rural people's ability to survive in harsh climatic, social, and economic conditions argued for the need to reassess and respect local knowledge and expertise.

Development agencies and university researchers began to devise processes, known as Rapid Rural Appraisal (RRA), which addressed the issue of how outsiders might gain knowledge and insights from rural people, while enabling local communities to have access to the results.[2] The use of survey question-naires, administered by external researchers, was seen to place a disproportionate value on factors that were quantitative rather than qualitative. It also tended to produce information that was biased by the social position, context, and gender of the respondents. And inevitably it reflected the cultural assumptions of the researchers. RRA methods, although still essentially extractive, marked an important step in development research methods, because their exponents posed the question: whose knowledge counts?

By the mid-1980s the terms 'participation' and 'participatory' were beginning to be used by development professionals in conjunction with RRA. It was claimed by the advocates of Participatory Rural Appraisal (PRA) — Robert Chambers and others — that the processes enabled farmers to become the principal 'owners' of information gained through a whole range of participatory methods, designed to enable villagers to focus on and discover things about their own lives and needs:

> A PRA process ... seeks to enable outsiders to learn, through the
> sharing of information in a manner which enhances people's analysis
> and knowledge and leaves them owning it ... for example, through
> participatory mapping of a watershed, where the map is used by
> villagers to plot current conditions and plan actions, and retained
> by them for monitoring action taken and changes; or through mapping
> and surveying degraded forest, deciding how to protect it and what to
> plant, and then managing the resource ... the aim is to enable people to
> present, share, analyse and augment their knowledge as the start of a
> process. The ultimate output sought is enhanced knowledge and
> competence, an ability to make demands, and to sustain action.
> Instead of imposing and extracting, PRA seeks to empower.[3]

In PRA, or PLA (Participatory Learning Approaches, or Participatory Learning and Action) as it is now generally known, the learning activities undertaken by local people in the local context are designed as a focus to promote critical thinking, and it is the discussion which such a focus provokes that leads to the real sharing of information and knowledge. Researchers use maps and diagrams drawn in dust on the ground, or group walks and discussions that take place along the routes familiarly taken to grazing grounds or water-sources, to enable women and men to share their knowledge of their own landscapes and to decide together the issues or topics they need to research further. From the global perspective of the whole village, they are able to discuss who owns which land, who produces what, which crops are best grown where, and so on. As a result, an overview of the social, economic, and environmental world of the village is built up by the village participants, and the focus of the later participatory research activities is developed from this perspective. The layers of the onion of village relations, conflicts, gender issues, health problems, wealth and poverty can gradually be peeled back and examined.

Problems with participatory approaches

A great deal of debate has focused on the definition and refinement of PRA/PLA processes and practices. At times it seems that there is an ever-expanding industry of participatory training and research. It is an industry that is not without its critics. David Mosse, for example, has warned that a set of given techniques is of secondary value to an understanding of the complex social and political environments in which they are applied.[4]

The mechanical application of PRA/PLA 'methods' or 'activities' (the mapping exercises, diagrams and so on) is one potential problem. Another is that the mere use of PRA/PLA methods is no guarantee that external bias will be eliminated and that local conditions — social, cultural, and political — will be respected. Researchers and project officers need extensive and sensitive training before they can safely use the methodology of PRA/PLA.

Often, far from producing an experience of mutual learning, initial PRA/PLA training gives trainees the impression that they are being asked to undertake a time-consuming piece of research with people of much lower educational standards than themselves. The information elicited from mapping and diagramming, it seems to them, could be produced more easily through conventional interviews. Often PRA/PLA is introduced as a one-off experience, and there is no chance for trainees to see it as one of a number of ways of working with villagers over an extended period. PRA/PLA is not a short-cut to information-gathering; rather, it is a long-term process involving sequences of learning and reflection between village people and outsiders. It is not always easy for trainees to appreciate that the aim of PRA/PLA is for villagers to undertake a progressive exploration of their own knowledge and contexts, in a way that elicits new insights and enables them to decide and 'draw down' the outside help and expertise they need. Such an approach requires flexibility as well as careful analysis of the outcomes of each day's activities, so that those of the following day can be understood and agreed by villagers as a progressive development and sharing of knowledge and planning throughout their community.

Another fundamental element of PRA/PLA, discussed in nearly every context as a potential pitfall, is the interpretation made by field-workers of the research and information produced by local people. There is a growing concern, among even the originators of participatory approaches in development, not only about the training of facilitators, but also about the organisational context in which PRA/PLA is operated. Robert Chambers writes of the operation of participatory approaches by field-workers within specific cultural contexts: 'Responsibility rests not in written rules, regulations and procedures, but in individual judgement.'[5]

PRA/PLA should be a flexible tool, yet much of the literature describes sets of checklists and methodologies. The handbooks, in their concentration on how to operate PRA/PLA methodologies, fail to emphasise that the most radical and also the most difficult aspect of PLA is that it should be used as a means of focusing, rather than determining, the topics of dialogue between participants. But this open-ended approach to the selection of topics or agendas, and the need for local people to appropriate or take over their own learning, fit awkwardly into the agendas and time-scales, logical frameworks, budget cycles, and report-writing demands of development agencies. The outcomes of PRA/PLA can and should be unpredictable. Inevitably there are tensions between local needs and the demands of funders and donors, who require reports to be submitted in a different language, in accordance with a schedule which may bear no relation to local realities. These are the considerations that have produced critical questions about where villager participation begins and ends.

Using participatory approaches in Vietnam

In the cultural and political context of Vietnam, there has been a great deal of debate about whether Participatory Rural Appraisal and participatory approaches to development are even possible.[6] Both the Confucian philosophy and the Marxist ideology are paternalist and authoritarian (though Marxism explains this as a temporary phase on the road to socialism).

A patrilineal and patrilocal kinship system reinforces Confucian principles throughout Kinh society in Vietnam. The influence of the Communist Party extends through local Party committees to national government. For Oxfam's staff in Vietnam, participation should and must include the participation of the government. As one member remarked: 'When we refer to community, we mean people and government together.'

In Vietnam, community participation in government is a traditional part of cultural life. But political and social custom describe the expression of individual difference as anti-social and counter-productive. By contrast, an essential feature of PRA/PLA is the exploration and definition of difference through wealth-ranking, gender analysis, and so on. In such a climate, will villagers in Vietnam be able to participate freely in research processes designed to enable them to set the agendas for their own development?

Participation and communication

Participation, representation, and communication by people on the margins of society, their relationship with government and with development agencies, and the ways in which such communications and representations are received and responded to are at the very heart of social development — but they also represent its weakest point. It is not only that the concepts are contested, but there are differing perspectives, too, about the levels of participation involved. Participatory approaches must lead us to question where participation begins and ends, and so to consider issues of representation and communication.

Development communications

It is interesting to note that the history of development communications has, like the history of development itself, thrown up a number of conflicting approaches to the issue of participation.

Melkote [7] has written critically about the 'bullet theory' of communication: the idea that radio broadcasts with development messages would create a climate of acceptance which could be followed up by extension workers. These 'agents of change' would provide detailed training in new techniques, together with resources to make modern innovations possible. It was a programme which had worked in Europe under the Marshall Plan, following the devastation of the second world war. The disappointing outcome of a similar programme to reach the poor of the South was put down to a strange failure to accept innovation and modernisation on the part of Third World peasants.

Although the 'bullet theory' of development communications was se essentially educational, it was the antithesis of contempora theories about participatory development, which, under the influence of Paulo Freire, were formulating new attitudes to the processes of teaching and learning in marginalised communities. Freire's 'pedagogy of the oppressed' claimed to enable poor and powerless people to break the 'culture of silence'. It linked a process of learning and teaching with action and reflection, leading to the development of a critical awareness about the way the world works. This Freirean critical pedagogy offered one of the keys to what is now known as the 'participatory learning' approach to development.

However, the failure of those involved in participatory development to engage with the spread of the mass media must be seen as a lost opportunity. It has meant that the alternative uses of such media for local representation have not been explored within the contexts of participatory development. It has led to a lack of imagination in the use of the technological by-products of the mass media, such as audio and video recorders, by development practitioners. The development of 'good practices' in relation to the participatory uses of the recorded media has been neglected.

Radio and television programmes designed to inform farmers and others through development 'messages' still represent a tiny proportion of broadcast media world-wide. Yet both radio and screen-based media have continued to reach rapidly expanding audiences, and, in the words of the media writer Tehranian, this has led to the 'globalisation of the local and localisation of the global'.[8]

How has this neglect of the development of the participatory uses of the media come about? What happened to Marshall McLuhan's grand claim that the new electronic media would create a 'global village', enabling the world's inhabitants to communicate directly with one another? The weakness of this concept is that it ignores the effects of a global system in which the consumers of programme content are simply at the bottom of the hierarchy of what has become known as 'the world information order'.[9]

At the same time, by ignoring the potential of the technological advances of the mass media for overcoming the barriers to communication posed by the need for written literacy, development professionals may have conspired in the abuse of the basic human right to freedom of expression. It could be argued that the ___ the media for minority representation neither begin nor end w__ ___ ___munications. Rather, clues to the media representation of ___ins of society lie in their uses of the spin-offs of high ___ all media of communication (video cameras, audio- ___pying machines, e-mail, and computers) are, as ___aking an equally powerful impact on revolutionary ___nents'.[10] He cites the non-broadcast use of video- ___eriods of resistance and change in Iran, South

A patrilineal and patrilocal kinship system reinforces Confucian principles throughout Kinh society in Vietnam. The influence of the Communist Party extends through local Party committees to national government. For Oxfam's staff in Vietnam, participation should and must include the participation of the government. As one member remarked: 'When we refer to community, we mean people and government together.'

In Vietnam, community participation in government is a traditional part of cultural life. But political and social custom describe the expression of individual difference as anti-social and counter-productive. By contrast, an essential feature of PRA/PLA is the exploration and definition of difference through wealth-ranking, gender analysis, and so on. In such a climate, will villagers in Vietnam be able to participate freely in research processes designed to enable them to set the agendas for their own development?

Participation and communication

Participation, representation, and communication by people on the margins of society, their relationship with government and with development agencies, and the ways in which such communications and representations are received and responded to are at the very heart of social development — but they also represent its weakest point. It is not only that the concepts are contested, but there are differing perspectives, too, about the levels of participation involved. Participatory approaches must lead us to question where participation begins and ends, and so to consider issues of representation and communication.

Development communications

It is interesting to note that the history of development communications has, like the history of development itself, thrown up a number of conflicting approaches to the issue of participation.

Melkote [7] has written critically about the 'bullet theory' of communication: the idea that radio broadcasts with development messages would create a climate of acceptance which could be followed up by extension workers. These 'agents of change' would provide detailed training in new techniques, together with resources to make modern innovations possible. It was a programme which had worked in Europe under the Marshall Plan, following the devastation of the second world war. The disappointing outcome of a similar programme to reach the poor of the South was put down to a strange failure to accept innovation and modernisation on the part of Third World peasants.

Although the 'bullet theory' of development communications was seen as essentially educational, it was the antithesis of contemporary pedagogic theories about participatory development, which, under the influence of Paulo Freire, were formulating new attitudes to the processes of teaching and learning in marginalised communities. Freire's 'pedagogy of the oppressed' claimed to enable poor and powerless people to break the 'culture of silence'. It linked a process of learning and teaching with action and reflection, leading to the development of a critical awareness about the way the world works. This Freirean critical pedagogy offered one of the keys to what is now known as the 'participatory learning' approach to development.

However, the failure of those involved in participatory development to engage with the spread of the mass media must be seen as a lost opportunity. It has meant that the alternative uses of such media for local representation have not been explored within the contexts of participatory development. It has led to a lack of imagination in the use of the technological by-products of the mass media, such as audio and video recorders, by development practitioners. The development of 'good practices' in relation to the participatory uses of the recorded media has been neglected.

Radio and television programmes designed to inform farmers and others through development 'messages' still represent a tiny proportion of broadcast media world-wide. Yet both radio and screen-based media have continued to reach rapidly expanding audiences, and, in the words of the media writer Tehranian, this has led to the 'globalisation of the local and localisation of the global'.[8]

How has this neglect of the development of the participatory uses of the media come about? What happened to Marshall McLuhan's grand claim that the new electronic media would create a 'global village', enabling the world's inhabitants to communicate directly with one another? The weakness of this concept is that it ignores the effects of a global system in which the consumers of programme content are simply at the bottom of the hierarchy of what has become known as 'the world information order'.[9]

At the same time, by ignoring the potential of the technological advances of the mass media for overcoming the barriers to communication posed by the need for written literacy, development professionals may have conspired in the abuse of the basic human right to freedom of expression. It could be argued that the uses of the media for minority representation neither begin nor end with satellite communications. Rather, clues to the media representation of those on the margins of society lie in their uses of the spin-offs of high technology. The small media of communication (video cameras, audio-cassette machines, copying machines, e-mail, and computers) are, as Tehranian points out, 'making an equally powerful impact on revolutionary and reformist social movements'.[10] He cites the non-broadcast use of video-cassette material during the periods of resistance and change in Iran, South

Africa, Eastern Europe, and the former Soviet Muslim republics. These 'alternative' uses of the new technologies indicate an acutely felt need for representation on the part of those who find themselves in situations of repression, as well as demonstrating their value for clandestine information-exchange and communication, and for the work of human-rights monitoring.

Representation and video

Video can enable under-represented and non-literate people to use their own visual languages and oral traditions to retrieve, debate, and record their own knowledge. Moreover, these recordings may enable excluded people to enter into negotiation with those in power over them, and to challenge the representations of others (even those within their own groups: the representation of the family offered by men, for example, might be challenged by women).

Practising representation needs to begin at village level, and to address the questions of who is being represented and who is listening. Villages are not homogeneous, conflict-free communities. They can be divided by class, caste, gender, wealth, power, and education. Using video to explore representation is valuable because, at one level, its pictures act as a mirror. Participants can see and hear themselves talking and they can retrieve what was said, in the way that it was said. They, and the facilitators of the process, can also notice who is absent. The picture can be discussed and analysed.

Community information in even the most participatory of PRA/PLA processes is usually not retrieved and represented before it is transformed. Often for purely practical reasons (because it will blow away or be obliterated), the drawing on the ground is copied on to paper, so that it can be pinned to a wall to facilitate feedback, sharing, and discussion with a wider group. What was a pebble on the ground becomes a dot on a piece of paper. The pebble was already a symbol, representing perhaps the score of a record rice harvest. Now it has changed again. The voices that described and commented on what it meant are gone. On paper it is only a dot. There is a danger that the score, as extractable hard information, becomes more dominant than any of the social issues discussed when the score was decided.

In fact, the pebble employed to represent a rice harvest on the ground had perhaps already introduced a form of literacy from outside, and now the vocabulary, the signs, and the code have been changed. These are variations in interpretations or literacies that go almost unremarked by many PRA/PLA practitioners. It is particularly in this area of the retrieval of information that video — despite the fact that it is still only 'an image of' the pebble — can eliminate some of the problems of this multiplication of codes. This is of particular concern where new literacies, such as diagramming, are introduced.

Teaching and learning with video

The focusing property of the camera can perform a function similar to that of the focusing tools used in traditional PRA/PLA — but the video recording retains more of the moment, in terms of the voices and the images of the participants. As a result, the processes of debate and learning on a chosen topic that may take place at village level can be retrieved more directly than when, for example, the graphic image of a diagram is copied from a drawing on the ground to a drawing on paper. Diagramming itself can become more dynamic, more culturally specific in terms of its visualisation, which is a consequence of the more flexible form of recording. The voices, explanations, and discussions that took place at the time are also recorded and can be retrieved by the participants.

In turn, the distancing function of the recording offers the viewer the opportunity to see and hear familiar everyday facts in a new way. The image framed on screen gains a new significance. The process of recording itself offers a wide range of possibilities, because it can both evoke the memory of the subject and provoke an imaginative reworking of it. For example, video makes it possible to imagine or act out choices: what would happen if young men understood that pestering girls for sexual favours destroyed young women's chances of getting on at school? In a Sudanese refugee camp, young men decided to act out the role of young women and so explore how it felt to be hassled. They recorded their drama on tape and showed it around the camp. A great deal of discussion was developed, involving not only other young men and women but also their parents.[11]

The processes of retrieving memory, debating issues, and imaginatively exploring them, supported by the participatory use of video, can enable marginalised people to reflect upon and produce their own representation. Significantly, video offers the means by which representation can be moved from one site of communication to another. Here, too, the process can be participatory and pedagogical, because recordings can be tested and monitored experientially in different contexts, by the participants themselves.

Some risks involved in using video

Despite its potential as a tool for participatory development, the use of video is subject to some of the risks we have already noted in connection with

PRA/PLA. It may, for instance, in the hands of development workers who fail to appreciate its real purpose, be used in a very mechanical way. Moreover, the use of video can encourage the imitation of the language and behaviour of professional TV or film crews, with a strong sense of their own importance and a hierarchical approach to the work of getting 'their' pictures and sound. By contrast, a participatory approach to video should aim to enable local participants to 'show' or 'tell' the camera the things that *they* decide to show and tell. In other words, direction should come from them, and they should use the camera as a tool to focus on the different aspects of their lives, as they wish. As in good PRA/PLA, villagers should select the agenda and use recordings to reflect on what they have said and shown. However, video is specifically valuable, because it can enable local participants to determine the forms of the showing and the telling — whether, for example, it is a dance, a drama, a story, or a song.

Behind these issues lie fundamental questions about what facilitators are facilitating. Are we training facilitators to perpetuate the use of method A or method B, or are we training them to facilitate the processes of unwrapping and restructuring knowledge so that local people can critically review their own lives? Are these processes concerned only with re-presenting local indigenous knowledge, or are they also about what Freire has called 'reading the world'? More importantly, perhaps, they are about accessing power, negotiating representation, and initiating communication.

The Ky Nam pilot project

Literacy, or the business of making and discerning meaning, can take many forms, from a song, to body decoration, to a wall-painting, or a message on the Internet. The Pilot Project on the Potential of Video as a Development and Campaign Tool was devised to test the value of using video for the retrieval and representation of information by local farmers in Vietnam, in ways which would enable them to speak and represent themselves directly (before their words were transformed into, for example, a written report). Video would be used primarily as a channel for research and the exchange of views and opinions among people who lived and worked in the same context. In addition, it was hoped to observe how the re-presentation of these video texts might be read by other groups or individuals whom the villagers chose to address. Staff in the Oxfam head office in Oxford also had the idea of seeking permission from local participants in Vietnam to use some of the material they produced as part of the presentations given annually at workshops for the British supporters of Oxfam's work.

As drafted by the Oxfam team in Vietnam, the original proposal for the pilot project had four main goals:

- to test the potential of video as a development tool with local village groups;
- to validate field-based learning through practice;
- to create a network of learning and exchange between players (villagers, development workers, and local authorities) at the local level;
- and to provide a potential source of exchange with other Oxfam programmes.

The proposal expressly left open the subject or subjects to be examined during the pilot project. In this sense the pilot project, which was directly funded by the Oxfam Vietnam programme, was intended to support a genuinely open agenda, to be determined by the participating farmers. The use of video implied from the beginning that the villagers would represent their own findings in their own voices.

A written report of their findings was not required. This meant that the project was not subject to paradoxical tensions, described by Christoplos, between the aims of PRA/PLA to empower the community to lead the process, and the needs of researchers to look subsequently for comparisons and variables through which to structure their written reports.[12] There was no requirement to justify the participatory experience in terms of a project cycle and investment, by translating information into outputs and task-oriented statements. This is not to say that PRA/PLA does not carry its own message to participating communities about potential outcomes, as well as about the identity of those who are initiating the activity. Both these aspects form essential findings of this case-study. Video also has its internal constraints, determined by time (the length of the tape), the manner of the filming, and the selection of points of view.

The training framework

The pilot project was framed within a three-week course of practical training in participatory video.[13] Three days were spent in Hanoi on team-building, acquiring basic technical skills, and receiving briefings from the Oxfam Vietnam team about conditions and issues in Ha Tinh Province and the Commune of Ky Nam. The training approach was informed by the obvious cultural diversity among the trainees themselves, who were drawn from four countries, with specialisms which included film, rural development, development communications, and women's union organisation. These differences made all the more apparent the need for the group to use this initial time together to address the issues of their own specific cultural and social composition, and to find ways of benefitting from this recognition of diversity.

Such self-analysis on the part of outsiders is essential. In this case, the 'outsiders' included the Vietnamese members of the group, who were as different from the villagers in background and education as were those who came from abroad. As the trainer, preparing the group for field-work, I regarded this analysis as no less important than the technical training in video skills or training in participatory approaches to learning. It was important, for example, for the group not to identify a hierarchy of technical production skills among themselves, because this would reduce the potential for handing over the direction of the video production to the village participants. For the field-work practice to enable villagers to appropriate the learning and determine the direction of the video, the approaches of the initial training workshop should offer a similar model. It should provide the opportunity for all members of the group to exercise judgement and to exchange roles and criticism freely.

At their preparatory workshop in Hanoi, the pilot-project participants met to agree aims and ground rules and to integrate their existing skills with video and participatory approaches. The majority of this group had not used video before. There were eleven members, consisting of three Oxfam Vietnamese project staff, one project worker from World Neighbors in Indonesia, one Canadian, five people from various organisations in Laos, co-ordinated by CIDSE, and a consultant in participatory video from the UK (see Table 2).

Diary of the pilot project

Phase 1

Days 1–4: Preparatory workshop in Hanoi, introducing participatory video, theory and practice, and practical edit-in-camera exercises. During this period the group also agreed aims for the project and drew up ground rules for working. The fourth day in Hanoi was used for briefings from Oxfam staff and for practical preparation for the field trip.

Phase 2

Day 5: The teams left in three vehicles for the ten-hour drive down Highway One to Ky Nam.

Day 6: Orientation and planning in Ky Anh at the District Offices and with the Commune officials of Ky Nam.

Day 7: Participation and observation in the three chosen villages.

Phase 3

Days 8–12: Participatory research, using video with villagers, and show-backs in the villages. In the evenings, the three teams shared their experiences and monitored and evaluated their performance.

Day 13: Rest day; editing

Day 14: Editing rough composite tapes to show back to all village participants at the evening 'editorial meeting'.

Phase 4

Day 15: Show-back discussion with villagers and commune leaders; planning with villagers for show-back to District Chairman.

Day 16: Show-back and review with Chairman in Ky Anh.

Day 17: Travel back to Hanoi.

Day 18: Evaluation in Hanoi.

Table 2: Participants in the pilot project

Name	Background in development and video	Nationality and organisation
Do Thanh Binh	Video worker and driver	Vietnamese; Oxfam UK/I Vietnam
Nguyen Minh Cuong	Project Officer	As above
Than Thi Thien Huong	As above	As above
I. V. Domingo	Development communications	Filipino; World Neighbors in Indonesia
Duongdi Khanthavilay	Interpreter	Lao; freelance
Haida Paul	Freelance film editor	Canadian; freelance
Viengmone Champasith Samuelson	Freelance film maker	Lao; freelance
Sengsoda	Women's organiser	Lao; Laos Women's Union
Chanthala Bouthavong	Project Officer	Lao; World Education
Phuvong Phetphayvanh	Camera operator	Lao; freelance
Su Braden	Consultant in participatory video for development	English; University of Southampton

The goals and structure of the pilot-project group

The workshop participants agreed the following goals when they first met in Hanoi:

- to learn basic video skills;
- to learn about participatory video methods;
- to choose with villagers a small participatory project and to use video to work on it together.

By the final day of the Hanoi preparatory workshop, the group had been able to divide into three teams, each headed by one Vietnamese speaker from Oxfam's participating staff, and with a good division between those who had some previous video experience and those who had none.

Team 1 consisted of Huong (the leader, who had no previous video experience), Haida (the most experienced editor), Viengmone (who had the most camera experience), and Sengsoda (who had previously had no video experience).

Team 2 was composed of Cuong (the leader, who previously had no video experience), with Chanthala (no previous video experience), and Phuvong (who had camera experience).

Team 3 contained Binh (the leader, who was Oxfam Vietnam's driver and the most experienced camera person), I.V. Domingo (known as 'I.V.', who had a little previous video experience, and good development communication skills), and Duongdi (who had no previous video or development experience).

Learning points from the preparatory workshop

From the three-day preparatory workshop in Hanoi, several learning points emerged. On the subject of team-building, we realised the importance of drawing up agreed aims; of drawing up and agreeing ground rules for working together; and of agreeing to share skills, languages, and local knowledge across the three teams who would work together in Ky Nam.

On the subject of giving and taking criticism, we learned the importance of offering constructive criticism when watching each other's tapes; and the need to help each other, to make the team as strong as possible. We used the device of listing and prioritising, to discover what behaviour created comfort or discomfort among group members.

Some concluding thoughts on representation

It has been said [13] that transparency in communication occurs when the flow between producer and receiver is not designed to conceal the interests of the sender. When communication is dominated by the desire to sell commodities, or ideology, it cannot be transparent. Mass communications are at the heart of market-based modernisation, with the consequence that programme content is merely a vehicle for advertising. NGOs concerned with what is rhetorically called empowerment ignore at their peril the power invested in centralised, exclusive control of mass communications. Yet changes in this power/ communications nexus are not easily achieved. Current political and economic forces have universally resulted in wider and wider distances being created between mass communications and the people whom they address. Practising representation, even at a village level, is a first step towards empowerment. Involving the authorities, even at the local level, is the next step. Such steps imply reclaiming the right to use the technology of communication, and redefining its use.

There is no point in practising conscientisation and participation for their own sakes: they must have outcomes. Sometimes the most significant outcome is an expression and exchange of views between the local community and the world beyond. Communication (including representation and response) is at the heart of what we like to think of as the democratic process. Progression towards claiming rights of representation must, of necessity, begin as a practice within small communities, where individuals learn to benefit from involvement and exchange, where the least-heard learn, and gain the right, to break the silence. But small communities also need to practise representing themselves in the wider world, and the players in the wider world need to be brought into this process.

The experience of the pilot project in Ky Nam would emphasise the specific realities of popular participation in representation for development.

Participant observation in Ky Nam 2

From outsider's information to insider's knowledge

While outsiders may always remain outsiders, a period spent in participating in village life can help to clarify the complex differences between the identities of outsiders and insiders. Participant observation can offer an opportunity for outsiders to observe how village life works, to appreciate that communities are not homogeneous, and to try to understand how power operates within village society. Crucially, it can offer insiders the opportunity to observe the outsiders and to decide whether they want to work with them.

It is easy to suppose that the outsiders are international NGO staff, employed both in the head office overseas and in the national office. Yet in Oxfam's Hanoi Office, where both local and international staff are employed, it might be assumed that, from the perspective of a Vietnamese villager, the local staff are not so much 'outsiders' as the ex-patriate staff are. And this is true ... to a certain degree. However, the local NGO staff, while speaking Vietnamese, and looking Vietnamese, are not villagers, nor necessarily do they originate from the region where any particular development project takes place. Their accents, their education, their clothes, and their cars will make the differences quite clear to the villagers.

Similarly, local authority staff, from the district or province, are outsiders to the villagers by reason of their salaried positions, education, power, dress, and so on.

All these outsiders are essential players in the establishment of a development project and, in order to get agreement to work with local people, all the players need to communicate with and to respond to one another.

This chapter will trace how knowledge about the Commune of Ky Nam was collected at various levels in this project, and how the information and priorities appeared to change, the closer the players got to the people themselves. It will also offer some indications of censorship within the village, and misinterpretations which were not picked up at the time, and which will be further discussed in the final chapters.

Briefing for field-work

The Commune of Ky Nam was chosen by the pilot-project team, in consultation with Oxfam Vietnam field staff and Country Representative, partly for logistical reasons — it had a conveniently placed guest house within easy reach of the villages — and partly because Oxfam had already conducted a short PRA/PLA in one of the villages (although no further work had been done there). Cuong, a Project Officer in the Oxfam team, had formed part of the PRA/PLA facilitation group in Minh Duc village; Huong, another Project Officer, and Binh, the Oxfam driver and video worker, had both visited the District on several occasions. Cuong had also been involved in the District proposals for a Schools and Trees project. Binh had participated with a Vietnamese film director in a film project about the sea dykes which Oxfam had financed in Ky Anh.

Oxfam UK and Ireland is currently involved in a number of other long-term projects in the District. It was as a result of this relationship of partnership and trust that the Country Representative had been able to approach the District Authorities and receive permission for the pilot project to be located in Ky Nam, and for video to be used in a collaborative way with the community.

On the last day of the pilot-project workshop in Hanoi, the teams were briefed by the Oxfam Country Representative and programme staff about Oxfam's work in Ky Anh District, and the findings of their previous PRA/PLA in the Commune of Ky Nam. The Country Representative ended his briefing by drawing the team's attention to a number of important points to be borne in mind while researching issues with the villagers. He stressed that the team should seek to involve a wide range of ages and both men and women; that they should look for issues in which communication could help advocacy; and finally that the team should let the people take the lead in selecting which issues were important to them.

The Commune of Ky Nam

The first day of the field-based part of the project in Ky Nam began with a programme of orientation: visits to the District Office in Ky Anh, to the Commune Committee in Ky Nam, and to various key vantage points around the commune itself.

The most important part of this orientation was the meeting with the Commune Committee. This enabled the team to cross-check some of the issues which had been raised in the briefing given by Oxfam staff in Hanoi and in the previous PRA. The commune officials explained that the commune had recently received a loan of 190,000,000 dong [1] from the German government

Su Braden

above Ky Nam Commune, viewed from the Ngang Pass.

to target the problems of poverty. As part of this programme they were currently preparing statistics on poor families. The presentation by the commune representatives, mostly male, was impressive. The commune building was a sparsely furnished room, and the workshop team sat around a long table, drinking tea from small china pots and bowls, with Huong and Cuong acting as interpreters.

The workshop teams concluded the day with a visit to the Ngang Pass, high above the commune, from where the river and the reservoir could both be seen. It was clear from there that the reservoir was lower than the fields it was supposed to irrigate. We could also see the three largest villages in Ky Nam Commune, including Minh Duc at the river mouth. Farther inland is Minh Tien, which is the site of the primary school for the whole commune, a newer settlement where some former Minh Duc families have been encouraged to move, to avoid the effects of salination and flooding at the river mouth; and Minh Quy, the most inland of the three and the closest to the government-built reservoir.

The commune is bounded on the landward side to the west and south by mountains, and to the east by the sea. Highway One cuts right through the commune, carrying all the country's north–south road traffic. The landscape, with its mountains, the sea, and its patchwork of (albeit dry) fields, is very beautiful.

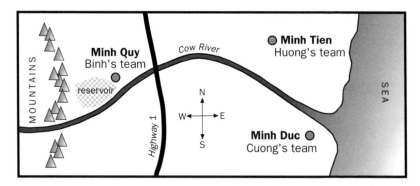

Participation observation [2] and feedback

The following day the three teams set off without cameras to spend some time participating and observing in the villages.

Minh Duc

In Minh Duc village, Cuong's team had cooked lunch with the head of the Women's Union. Phuvong went to the market for food for lunch. He noted that the kitchen was very clean and that the woman had used the minimum of firewood for cooking. She used water from the irrigation canal for drinking. The team took their afternoon nap in her house after eating. Then they visited two other families and walked with them across the village to their fields. They walked along a very low dyke beside the river, noticing that the sluice gates were in a bad state of repair and that the ponds created for aquaculture were dirty, so that the water could not circulate.

Minh Tien

In Minh Tien, Huong's team spent time talking mostly with women. They found that the village produced two rice crops per year, but that only the winter crop was reliable. Thirty newly settled families who had moved from Minh Duc in 1991 were doing a lot of construction work, organised communally, in the slack part of the year.

The team took a child suffering from a dog bite to the clinic. They found that the most frequently treated illness was malaria, but they were not able to ascertain whether people paid for medicine.

They spoke to a widow with two children, who said she could not attend the Women's Union meetings because she was on her own. She also said she was afraid to join the community credit schemes, because she did not feel she could repay the money.

Oxfam/Keith Bernstein

Oxfam/Sean Sprague

above A sea dyke in Ky Anh District.
below The clinic in Ky Nam.

Later in the day, Huong's team visited the primary school, where they learned that there were 300 children in the commune but that 100 had dropped out of school. The headmaster, Mr Tuy, claimed that the school management was not good at the commune level and that they provided no funds for school books.

Minh Quy

Binh's team in Minh Quy visited twelve families. They found it a problem that the village headman had at the beginning offered to act as their guide and tended to answer their questions on behalf of the villagers. However, the team reported later that they had done their best to participate in the life of the village by helping them to drink tea and wine! Issues raised by Minh Quy villagers included the pressing problems of water and irrigation; and also credit and loans: people were worried about repayments, especially the very poor. I.V. reported that they had spoken to one woman bringing up five children on her own, who told her that the village headman, Mr Linh, had personally guaranteed her loan, and that this had enabled her to earn a small income from making rice wine. She uses the waste material to feed her pigs.

Key issues

That evening at the guest house, the members of the three teams shared their experiences of the day, and produced charts from the information they had gathered, cross-checking issues raised with those of the previous day's briefings, and the Hanoi briefing. The idea was that each team would take this information back to the villagers and suggest looking further into one or more of what seemed to the villagers to be the most important issues.

The first two days had offered the teams interesting insights into the problems and challenges of field research. The briefings they had received in Hanoi and from the Commune and the District authorities had all dealt with similar issues, but in the villages the emphasis had seemed, after only one day, slightly different.

Migration

The Oxfam Hanoi team and the Commune Committee had expressed concern about migration trends in the area: both temporary and permanent migration was taking place, in line with the Provincial plan to move people south to Dak Lak Province, to live and work in the New Economic Zone. Community leaders reported that 40 households had moved south to the rubber plantations, but recently five had returned because of a malaria epidemic. Young people migrated seasonally to work on harvests in other Provinces, but they usually returned to the Commune.

Despite the emphasis placed on migration in the official briefings, during the day of participant observation no villager mentioned it as a pressing problem.

Fisheries and aquaculture

The Oxfam team in Hanoi saw aquaculture as potentially the most rewarding activity for the commune, because of the great demand for crabs and shrimps. They identified the constraints on fishery development to be the lack of capital and equipment, and the damage caused by frequent storms. They noted that people from the neighbouring Quang Binh Province travel to Ky Nam Commune to fish, with their bigger boats and better equipment.

The Commune Committee was concerned about economic losses caused by diseases spread by the semi-intensive conditions of aquaculture. Among the eight households in the commune which had their own shrimp and crab ponds, average losses amounted to three million dong per family.

The villagers were not convinced that aquaculture could become a viable form of income-generation. They were very concerned about problems of flooding and contamination: the sand-bar that had formed at the mouth of the river was trapping salt water in the river, which was flooding the surrounding land.

below A fishing boat in Ky Anh District.

Oxfam/Keith Bernstein

The impact of the war

The Oxfam Hanoi briefing stressed the problem of exploding ordnance left behind after the American war. (The Ho Chi Minh Trail starts here, and roads and bridges were under constant attack during the war.) The Commune Committee were also concerned about the problems of land mines and other ordnance, but stressed in addition the prevalence of genetic deformities thought to be associated with the use of Agent Orange during the war: two malformed children, in the same family, had died within the last year.

For the villagers questioned during the day of participant observation, the main problem associated with the war was the oppressive presence in the commune of an American Missing in Action (MIA) team, based in a substantial MIA camp at the mouth of the river outside Minh Duc. Some villagers were being paid to search the hillsides for missing planes, which gave rise to considerable bad feeling. Rumours of misconduct were rife: one of the Americans was accused of spitting in a village well.

Land distribution

The Hanoi team was concerned about the fact that rice fields had been distributed to individuals, but that these people had no official title deeds to their plots. The Commune Committee was at pains to stress the fairness of the allocation procedures. For the villagers, the question of land distribution was overshadowed by the issues of irrigation and salination.

below Strengthening a sea dyke in Ky Anh district after a typhoon.

Oxfam/Ben Fawcett

Salination and water supply

These were issues which greatly preoccupied both the Commune Committee and the villagers. All blamed the sand-bar which has formed across the river mouth, trapping the salt floods in the river, and forcing the river to overflow the dykes and inundate the fields. The system of irrigation canals was not working properly, and the reservoir walls needed raising, to improve the storage and flow of water. There were problems which had been raised with the District Government many times. They did not feature in the briefing given in the Oxfam office in Hanoi.

Natural disasters

Neither the Hanoi team nor the Commune Committee mentioned the problem of typhoons, but the villagers were troubled by the damage done to their houses and crops.

Education

The Oxfam briefing identified the lack of a secondary school as one of the Commune's main problems. The Commune Committee agreed, but also cited the problem of non-attendance at primary school: of 300 children of primary-school age, 100 were not turning up at the school which Oxfam had built. The villagers did not, as expected, ask for a secondary school, but did raise the problem of non-attendance at the primary school, suggesting that the reasons should be investigated.

Begging and prostitution

Oxfam field-workers noted that beggars and prostitutes (known euphemistically as 'faded flowers') were a frequent sight on Highway One. The Commune authorities admitted that begging was a problem, and one which they had already raised with the authorities in Hanoi. The Committee said that the 'faded flowers' were not from their area; and claimed that child prostitution on Highway One was no longer a problem.

The villagers denied seeing any beggars, but angry parents alleged in Minh Quy that a national television crew, making a documentary film about children begging on the Highway, had rounded up children to pose for the cameras. No villagers mentioned the issue of 'faded flowers'.

Introducing participatory research

The next morning, the **Minh Tien** team took a camera to the village for the first time and worked with a group of women, men, and children. They began by getting everyone to record each other, and then playing back short pieces of tape. Then they initiated an informal conversation about school fees and the problem of school drop-outs. They showed the tapes back to the group, who expressed themselves happy with what they had said. However, some of the discussion concerned the filming itself, and two women, Mrs Tham and Mrs Dung, told the team that they did not like seeing themselves on screen, especially in close-up, when they felt that the camera was 'burning' their faces.

Meanwhile, in **Minh Quy**, Binh's group had spent the morning with an old woman, whom they filmed drawing a map of the village and describing the water shortage. She told them that especially in the summer months, when the two village creeks dry up, there is no water for the crops. In the afternoon, Binh's team used this recording to generate discussion with a wider group of villagers. The map made by the old woman had been drawn directly on to the sand, and other villagers pointed out that it was not clear, and that the explanation had been incorrect in some details. Binh used this criticism to ask whether the villagers could produce a more detailed version, and to suggest that they did it using sticks and stones to make it more three-dimensional. The villagers were clearly puzzled by this concept, and appeared reluctant. Binh responded by explaining how the contours and shadows produced by three-dimensional objects would be seen more clearly by the camera. He and the team collected a selection of stones to represent houses, small leafy twigs to represent forest, and so on; they laid them out on the ground and filmed them. They demonstrated the effect on the monitor, and asked the villagers whether they thought this image was clearer. This demonstration brought an immediate enthusiastic response, and the villagers said that by the next morning they would have built a detailed model which would show all the houses and fields of the village, the reservoir, the creeks, and the irrigation scheme.

A young man jumped up and made an angry intervention. It was all very well to build a model, he said, but no one ever listened to the problems of the village, neither the Commune Committee nor the district authorities. Other villagers stepped in and said that Oxfam was neither the commune nor the district, and argued that they should take time to discuss their problems with these visitors.

The **Minh Duc** team spent the day showing a camera to villagers in small family groups and recording semi-structured interviews. They also worked with a group who made an improvised model with wooden planks on the ground to show the shape of the river mouth. The villagers demonstrated how a sand bank had formed that blocked the river, and they explained that the dykes along the river bank were too low to prevent the trapped sea-water flooding over into their rice fields.

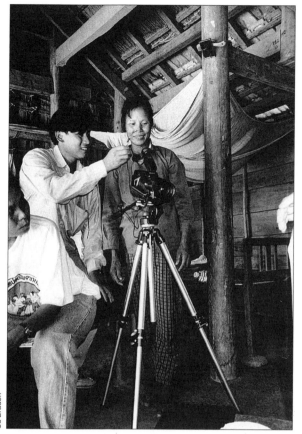

left A demonstration of camera techniques in Minh Duc.

Su Braden

'Cinema sessions': group learning

The pilot-project team lived and ate together, and often shared a swim in the sea before the evening meal. The swim became an important event which enabled the teams to relax together and get to know each other in a context away from the work. This meant that people felt good about working after supper at the evening 'cinema' meetings, in which each team presented their day's work. The TV monitor was set up on the back steps of the guest house, and the team set up chairs and trays of tea, using torches to 'spotlight' speakers as they introduced the work they had done that day. It became an enjoyable end-of-the-day event, in which eventually many of the villagers joined as well, despite having already watched the same material earlier in the evening.

On this first occasion, the complaints about close-up shots made by the women in Minh Tien were useful, because they enabled the trainer to discuss with the teams the problem of framing, and the power that this invests in the camera operator to decide what information and what opinions to include or exclude. It was agreed that each team should take care to show villagers how framing is done. The example of Binh's team's experience with the two forms of mapping demonstrated a way of asking villagers to decide their preferences.

The other issue that arose was the risk of asking leading questions. Some people felt that the Minh Tien group had been in danger of leading the Minh Tien women in their criticism of the primary-school staff.

Conclusions

It can be seen that the role of the outsiders in this introductory phase of the pilot project had an energising effect. But this is a phase where great sensitivity is clearly needed. There is a need for transparency, to establish not only the meaning of what is being said, but the identities and motives of the speakers. In Ky Nam, the teams introduced themselves and explained their presence as part of a longer-term Oxfam commitment to 'the district'. They explained that, in this instance, they had come to test and learn from using a new medium for research with the villagers, and that they would need the villagers' help and advice. In retrospect, this explanation was probably not as transparent to the villagers as the team had intended it to be. To the team, the definition of 'district' meant generally the whole of the Ky Anh District, including, but not specifically, Ky Nam. They were referring to a general commitment to a wide geographical area in terms of support for a number of different projects, including those currently funded by Oxfam UK and Ireland in Ky Anh, such as education projects. But (as it later turned out) 'district' was understood by the villagers as relating to their own particular geographical location. Given the pressing problems that they were experiencing, it was later clear that some villagers, at least, may have interpreted this general commitment as a commitment to meet the specific needs which they later expressed on video.

It was explained that none of the material recorded would be shown elsewhere without the permission of the villagers, individually and collectively. The presence of foreigners, who were new to Vietnam, helped to underline the real need for learning on the part of the pilot team, and made clear the need for questions and for translation. This 'foreignness' was clearly apparent to all those who came into contact with the teams during the participant observation day. On this day, the outsiders were in need of guidance and help from the villagers. They needed instruction in what must have appeared to the villagers as the everyday business of survival: how to find their way about, where and how to get water or buy food to eat, and so on. At the same time, this 'foreignness' allowed the outsiders to ask questions and to cross-check some of the views they had gained about the village from beyond the village, and from the authorities within the village.

Participant observation enables the outsiders to become visitors and offers the villagers individual choices about inviting them into their homes. Where these invitations are made, the visitor has a natural responsibility to show interest in the everyday concerns of the host.

There was discussion during team feedback sessions about the status of the people whom the teams were meeting and the degree to which they represented the village populations. The political context of the pilot project meant that participation had, indeed, to include 'people and government'. Yet at this stage it was not always clear in the village context who was who. The people could not participate at all without the consent of the Party Committee and the local authorities. Inevitably this consent involved controls and monitoring, and it would probably not be clear how these controls operated until some time later, nor whether they should be the concerns of a project whose brief was to enable people 'to practise representation'. The conclusion of the discussion was that practice makes perfect, and that we were only at the threshold of introducing a new skill into a long-established cultural context. We needed to be conscious of who was participating, but the implications would take time to emerge.

above Villagers in Minh Quy reviewing a rough edit of their tape.

Su Braden

Participatory research and analysis in Ky Nam   3

Generating and sharing information in Minh Tien

The Minh Tien team, later known as 'the education team', used the day after the first evening cinema session to show the interviews recorded the previous day with a small group, mainly women, to a larger meeting in Minh Tien village. The tape that had been produced on the first day was now used by the team to facilitate further discussion. A snowball process of accumulation had begun, and the views and testimonies of the first group about alleged corruption in the primary school produced new information from the viewers. One woman commented:

> The land around the school is given to the teachers by the
> Commune for their extra income. It's their land and they should
> work it themselves. Why do they use the children's labour? When grass
> clearing is needed, they make them clear grass. In the harvesting season
> they make them harvest. It's excessive. As far as I am concerned, I think
> the teachers are going too far.

A second woman added her view:

> Sometimes it's too much. For example, it's OK for the big kids to
> work, but these small ones sometimes have to go to collect wood for
> fences and firewood for the teachers.

The two women who had complained about close-ups the previous day remained to take part. Mr Nong suggested showing the tape to the headmaster. Although some people appeared reluctant, or too busy to go, others agreed, and said they would be at the school at 3 pm, to show the headmaster the views of the Minh Tien parents, and to have a discussion about their suspicions.

An appointment was made with the headmaster for 3 pm. But only one person from the morning discussions, Mr Nong, turned up. The headmaster, with his female administrator and a male school manager, offered everyone tea. The team, with Mr Nong, went ahead and showed the tapes. The headmaster reacted angrily and said that the people had incorrect information. The team offered to record his answers to the questions raised about the labour rules for primary schools, the money which the children were told to bring to school, and the firewood they had to collect.

The headmaster recorded in his reply that money requested from the children had been used to pay for rice for a school party, tea for visitors to the school, and books. Drinking their tea, the team took note! However, he agreed to a meeting with the villagers and added that it was a breakdown in communication between schools and parents that was at the root of these misunderstandings.

The evening cinema discussion

The teams were all aware that the work of the 'education team' in Minh Tien, and the charges of corruption that parents were making against the primary school, were of a different order of complexity from the practical issues encountered by the Minh Duc and Minh Quy teams.

The evening 'cinema' discussions, now attended by villagers as well as the members of the pilot-project team, came to the conclusion that there should be some strategy for conflict-resolution. Some team members felt that perhaps the Minh Tien team had rushed the show-back to the headmaster.

The discussion was led by the other Oxfam Vietnam field-workers, who consulted the villagers present and suggested that the education group should cross-check all the information they had gained about the corruption charges against the primary school. Cuong, Huong, and Binh agreed that it was crucial to avoid the possibility of recriminations and further threats to parents or children who had spoken out, either at the time or after the team's departure. Equity of access to the process of using video to facilitate communication between the various groups was seen as the most important ingredient of this process, because information hitherto contained within the private world of the families was being offered in the public domain. The team's main concern was that the process of village representation, by posing a threat to the reputation of the headmaster, risked provoking an oppressive response from the authorities. The evening 'cinema' discussions concluded that, while the need for transparency demanded that both sides should be given equal opportunities to use the platform offered by the video process, it would be important to encourage the school, commune, and district authorities to see the participation of parents in discussing the problems of the school as healthy. This discussion itself took place in debate with the villagers present, and they made it clear that they were happy for others to be consulted.

As in the village context, the tapes were used, in this case by the teams themselves, to generate their own analysis and debate. The villagers present agreed that the Minh Tien team should go to the village of Minh Duc the following day to show both the parents' tape and the headmaster's reply, and to collect a wider range of views.

Research and analysis in Minh Duc

The Minh Duc group spent the morning of the first day of participatory research showing back the interviews and rough model of the river-mouth from the previous day, and using the discussions that arose from the feedback to prioritise with the villagers the problems to be worked on for the remaining period of their visit. Villagers decided that their first priority was to look at the reasons behind the formation of the sand-bar across the river-mouth and the flooding that resulted. It was this salt water that was destroying their livelihood. Table 3 represents the villagers' analysis of the causes of the problem of sea-water flooding.

Table 3: Minh Duc villagers' analysis of the problem of sea-water flooding

The sand-bar at the river-mouth	The existing dykes	Income-generation
'The estuary is blocked because of the north-east wind, and it is usually blocked from March.'	'Let me explain the situation of Minh Duc village. There are fields on the northern and southern sides of the river … high and strong tides come into this river and run over the small dykes (along the river bank), and the two fields are seriously flooded.'	'The blocked river-mouth affects everything. First of all, the sea-water is trapped and cannot be released; it floods and affects the rice fields. Secondly, shrimps and crabs, the most valuable products, cannot get into the river-mouth. Thirdly, the fishing boats do not have a way to land.'
'It's very difficult to take my boat to and from the sea, because this (river) mouth is blocked by sand. We have to disassemble the motor and the nets, and it takes about eight people to carry this boat. Our difficulty is that the blocked river-mouth does not permit the boats to go in or out.'	'The dyke [indicating along the river bank] is too low. It doesn't stop the water from flooding over in high tides.'	'Along the dykes, people wish to make more ponds for shrimps and crabs, which have a very high export value.' 'In Minh Duc, we live mainly on agriculture. Besides that, we also live on fishing in the sea: shrimps, crabs, and octopus. It's much more profitable than agriculture, but is vulnerable.' 'These fields are flooded every year by salt water coming up the river and flooding over the dyke. That's why rice cannot be planted. Only wild grass can grow.'

A large crowd had gathered around a more sophisticated model. It included the river-mouth, the sand-bar, and the fields on both sides of the river, as well as the existing dykes and sluices. It had been decided to use the model to try to find a technical solution to the problem of sea-water flooding. Although there were many women in the crowd, a group of about five men took turns in using a short stick to discuss proposals for how they would resolve the problem, by diverting the currents that were produced by the flood tides, and preventing the sand-bar from building up. People in the crowd contributed, but the occasion was dominated by the men, perhaps because men are more accustomed to attending and expressing their views at meetings, or because the technical topic was seen as their domain.

Table 4 represents the solutions produced by the villagers as a result of their discussions about the model of the river-mouth. The solutions reflect their assessment that income-generation (i.e. survival) depends on solving the problem of flooding.

Reflections with the Minh Duc team about facilitation and filming

The Minh Duc trainee team had decided democratically to share the camera work throughout this long discussion. They had tried to cover practically the whole morning's event, and were concerned to use the camera unobtrusively. Yet when the tapes were shown back at the evening 'cinema', they received a critical verdict from the other two teams, who were clearly disappointed that, while so much had been achieved by making the model of the river-mouth, the documentation did not offer a 'readable' record. Many of the shots had been taken by the most inexperienced camera people in the team. Instead of clarifying the event and the discussions, the edit-in-camera technique had resulted in what seemed to be a very confusing documentation of the morning's work.

It was clear at this stage that Cuong, although the most experienced development worker in his group, had not yet had enough video experience to appreciate the need to co-ordinate his team's filming at the same time as facilitating the villagers' research. By assuming that the camera should be unobtrusive, the team had not enabled the villagers to take control of what was filmed, and to consciously 'show' the camera what they wanted recorded. As a result, the event was recorded in an incoherent way.

Much of the necessary material was there, but it would now need to be put into sequence, and to be cross-checked with the villagers. The trainer suggested using the following morning to review the Minh Duc tapes a second time with Cuong's team, and to select sequences with them, in the form of a rough edit, to give some coherence to the material they had collected. For this

Table 4: The solutions proposed by villagers to the sea-water flooding at Minh Duc

Proposals	Discussion	Solution
'I want to block (the river-mouth) and put a sluice underneath (the block).'	'There are usually heavy rains. If we block the mouth, the dam will need to be very high.'	'One solution is to bank up the two sides of the mouth. Another solution is to bank the mouth and have a sluice. It should work well in the flood season.'
'The authorities suggest a breakwater at the mouth. ... We should build a breakwater. It should be concrete, and it will prevent the sand from coming into here [indicating the river-mouth], and the sea-water can come in and out freely. The rocky foot of the mountain will be like the second natural embankment.'		
'This [indicating the river Cow] is a canal for outgoing water. We should dredge it and make a sluice here. The flood-water from upstream would go through this sluice and water from here (sea-water) would also go through with sluice.'	'So we should dredge this canal. If you make a sluice without dredging, it will be useless.'	
'The two dykes should be strengthened to prevent the sea-water flooding over into the fields. If you block the river-mouth, we will lose the natural fish that come into the river. We should consider the economic benefits. We should dredge this river 2m – 3m deep, and then build a breakwater and raise the dam slopes. It will benefit the two fields; and the boats can anchor here and the fish can come in.'		'To benefit both the fields and the fisheries, we should dig the river and build the breakwater. If the sand comes in, it will be useless.'

process the tapes were played directly from the camera into a domestic video-tape recorder, recopying the sequences that recorded how the villagers had developed their analysis of the problem and the solution of the sea-water flooding. From this material it was clear that the villagers understood the cause of their problems and that, by using an improvised model of the river-mouth, they had found a good technical solution to the build-up of sand. They had recommended using an angled sea dyke, which would stop the current

45

Table 5: Problems as analysed from their map by Minh Quy villagers

Natural resources	Irrigation	Reservoir	Income-generation
'A mountain stream provides good water during part of the year.' 'There is plenty of water from August onwards. From February to August there is none.' 'In the rainy season there is plenty of water in the fields anyway.' 'In the dry season we can do nothing in our fields.' 'The wells also dry up in the dry season.'	'The canal system is very short.' 'The canals here were built by Ky Nam people, under the guidance of a technician, but are now much lower than the fields, and so they fail to give irrigation, and the water just runs out to the sea.'	'The reservoir was built a long time ago with foreign funding, and under the management of the Party. It is not helping us, because the two streams running into it are dry in this season. The reservoir bed is filled with fallen trees, rocks, and earth that have remained there since the floods. There has been no maintenance since the day it was built.'	'We cannot live from agriculture. We cannot become rich from rice. We need to develop other income-generation activities, such as aquaculture, fisheries, and livestock. The thing we need most now is a loan.'

backing up against the rocky foot of the mountain. They saw that the mountain itself would prevent the sand drifting when the current changed direction. They had also recommended that the dykes along the river bank should be raised, to prevent flooding during the typhoon season.

A first attempt at using video for participatory research in Minh Quy

The same day, the Minh Quy group returned to the village to find that a very detailed village model had been made, and the team were able to record a comprehensive explanation of the irrigation problems and problems of income-generation that arose as a result. Table 5 shows the problems analysed by the villagers of Minh Quy from their map.

The discussion of the map, and indeed the act of showing their village and their problems to outsiders, led to a good deal of reflection about ways in which problems arose, and specifically about issues of management. It enabled the villagers to begin to distinguish those problems which they could solve themselves from those for which they needed outside assistance. The young

Table 6:
Solutions offered by Minh Quy villagers to the problems they had defined

Natural resources	Irrigation	Reservoir	Income-generation
'There is no one to save water — to love water. The water is left running wastefully, and the consequence is that there is no water in the summer. We should not just blame the authorities. Nature is not fully to blame either. Humans must bear over fifty per cent of the fault.'	'There is an over-flow weir to let the water go in the stormy season. I think that the technical designers have made the canals too deep, and there is no one to protect and maintain the water source.' 'This over-flow weir should also be repaired and up-graded.'	'I am a backward peasant woman, but I have a wish to have the reservoir and the canal. That's enough. And also if there is money, we should have pumping machines to pump the water from the reservoir.' 'To have water in the dry season, the dam's bank should be raised, and this goose-neck sluice should be repaired and the canals should be up-graded. To supply water for the lower fields on the other side of the road, the dam should be raised and a "floating" canal along the foot of the pass will take water into that field.'	It was noted that at this stage no solutions were offered. Only later, after seeing the first rough edit of the complete tape, women suggested adding material on income-generation.

man who had been so angry the previous day now took on an active and creative role, and used the map to look at the problems of irrigation and water-storage. The village headman, who was also a representative of the People's Committee, still played a prominent role, but others, including women, also spoke, and a crowd of some fifty villagers remained throughout the discussion. Table 6 shows the solutions discussed by villagers in Minh Quy to the problems of irrigation and water-storage which they had defined.

The evening had been taken up by the discussion of the Minh Tien team's education issues, and with the technical filming problems encountered by the Minh Duc team, but the tapes were reviewed with a wider group of Minh Quy villagers the following morning.

Commentary

If a sensitive balance can be struck between outsider and insider knowledge, the outsiders can enable the insiders to explore and record their knowledge in a way that makes it freshly available to them, and useful for their own critical analysis. The teams had already gained some useful experience of this process.

In **Minh Quy**, the use of the video to record and play back the villagers' discussions arising from the village model had offered the villagers the opportunity to understand how to direct the camera to record and retrieve their own information. This process, in turn, enabled them to expose a critical view of the problems of water-storage and irrigation. It remained to be seen how they would use this information, and whether they might decide to separate the problems for which they would be able to take responsibility from those for which they would need to appeal for outside help. Some of the information produced revealed their need to communicate better with each other, while other information showed that they needed to address authorities or advisers beyond the village.

It was clear that the headman in Minh Quy was managing the relationship between the team and the village, but the intervention of the angry young man on the first day gave some indication that there were other views. It would have been interesting to know whether his cooperation on the second day was the result of 'a word from the headman', or whether he had simply changed his view about the value of the research being proposed by the outsider team.

The problems which had occurred with filming in **Minh Duc** highlighted the importance of making the filming process available to the villagers, to enable them to direct the recording of the information that they will wish to retrieve.

Participatory approaches to community development are generally based on a number of assumptions about people's knowledge and people-led development. The danger is that participation can expose vulnerable people to oppression. Notions of participation are not only political [1] in terms of government and NGO policy: they are also cultural. Interventions that seek people's participation are dynamic processes which include aspects of people's relationships to government, as well as the relationship or control exercised by government. From this perspective, the processes can be seen as pedagogical, both in the context of the village and with the players beyond the village. There is a need to offer both people and authorities safe ground on which to practise these new forms of exchange.

The development of village narratives

The following afternoon, the **Minh Duc** team showed to the villagers the information they had retrieved from the recordings of the model of the river-mouth. During the next three days villagers formed an editorial group and discussed with the visiting team the additional material needed to create a tape which they could use in advocacy to argue for the construction of a new sea dyke. The villagers set up additional interviews and found suitable locations from which the problems caused by salt-water flooding could be filmed.

They introduced the team to an elderly farmer who had written a song about the problem. It was decided to use his song as the introduction to the film:

> *... who passes by the windy Ngang Pass,*
> *the sea water floods the rice field*
> *and the stormy water rises.*
> *The land is inundated*
> *and all the labour of ploughing*
> *and harrowing is wasted ...*

The formation of a village editorial group, and their selection of material and interviews to be filmed, occupied the remaining days. The village group decided to present an argument for their own solution to the problem of salt-water flooding, using the video team as a technical resource for their presentation. They hoped that this film would be shown to the authorities and to potential funders.

Minh Quy also formed a village editorial group, as a result of the show-back and discussions provoked by the tape of the new village model. The trainee team regularly re-played footage to the villagers, who worked out what material was needed next. The team organised a rough edited version of all the material to date, to show back to the village at a large meeting attended by the whole workshop and all the villagers. Here, the village women suggested that, although the problem of water-storage and irrigation was at the root of Minh Quy's poverty, the film so far did not show the effect of this on income-generation, and on the survival of women and children. It was decided that a further section should be added to explore how women were surviving now, and what their aspirations were for the future.

The exchange of roles between the pilot-project team, as outsiders introducing the use of video for village research, and the village editorial groups using it for their own representation indicates an important change in the ownership of the processes introduced. While the technical management of the equipment remained in the hands of the pilot teams, the villagers took over its direction, made changes, discussed new sequences to be set up, and decided how they to be were framed. The agreement between the pilot team and individual participants, about what was shown to wider audiences within the village, was seen to be honoured. The proposal by the women in Minh Quy for the additional footage about income-generation appeared to indicate their growing confidence in the video process.

above Tug of war at Ky Nam primary school.

Oxfam/Sean Sprague

Conflict: the private and the public

4

Definitions of 'public' and 'private' spheres

In asking what was happening in Ky Nam, the outsider might have felt it was almost presumptuous to pose the question in such a way that it elicited more than just a list of material problems: 'The sea water is flooding our fields ... we have a problem with irrigation ... there is no secondary school'. Private problems of a domestic nature, or problems of community conflict, are less easy to talk about — and often less easy for the community itself to understand in terms of cause and effect. Talking about such problems may also be seen as unsafe, running the risk perhaps of further discrimination or oppression. Yet modern psychology tells us that such problems can be helped by talking to an outsider and thus making discussion more objective.

It might be thought that in the Vietnamese context the presence of a video camera would discourage people from talking about private issues. The technology is still closely associated in most people's minds with the mass media. Significantly the social and economic transition taking place in Vietnam in the second half of the 1990s is reflected in changes in ways in which people are defining their understanding of the private and public spheres. In capitalist society, material reproduction (institutions, money, power) is seen as the function of the State and represents the public sphere, while the private sphere is inhabited by the worker and the consumer. The communist States drew the lines differently. In Vietnam — until *doi moi*, at least — the worker/consumer and his or her family were part of the public sphere. The public sphere was assumed to subsume the private, and that which was truly private risked being seen as anti-State.

In capitalist society, and in the commercial media, the definitions of the public and private spheres are more easily and voluntarily transgressed. And yet in these societies too, both spheres are cultural as well as political.

In both contexts, by re-examining and introducing the technology of representation, such as video, for alternative uses and practices, and by ensuring that those who speak have ultimate control over decisions about who beyond the immediate group will see and hear what they have said, a video recording becomes a tool through which the group itself can retrieve what has

51

been said. The decision to talk about sensitive subjects can be taken with this insurance in mind. Yet, as the participants watch and hear film of themselves being replayed in their own small groups, self-confidence grows. They can make the decision to move the discussion from the privacy of their own group, to test reaction to what they have said in a more public forum of their own choosing. Sometimes this second forum will be, as in the case of Ky Nam, parents like themselves, in another part of the commune. In this second forum, the second group may add their comments, or contribute more evidence to what the first group has said. Again, confidence may or may not be gained, and the larger group may once more discuss whether this material should be shown elsewhere — even to the authorities. They may also choose which parts of the material should be shown to a specific audience.

In Ky Nam, until the arrival of the pilot-project team, the alleged corruption in the only primary school in the Commune had been discussed mainly in the privacy of family homes, among parents. They feared for the progress of their children in the new Vietnamese economic climate. The opportunity afforded by the video project, and the fear that the children were being victimised, led them to see the interest of the family as separate from that of the school belonging to the Commune. So the parents decided to move the issue from the private sphere into the public sphere, despite their awareness of the risks involved.

The headmaster is called to account

The parents in all three villages were now consulted about the problems in the primary school. The education team went to Minh Duc and showed the tapes made by parents in Minh Tien, and the headmaster's reply. They filmed four women gathered with their children in one house, who confirmed, with an even stronger emphasis, the reports of the parents from Minh Tien. The Minh Duc parents said that their own children had been threatened by the teachers, who made constant demands that even five-year-olds should bring bundles of wood and baskets of dung to school. They claimed they had been told that they could not attend unless they produced money, firewood, or dung. One woman claimed:

> ❮ Anyone who doesn't have the kind of grass needed to make sweeping brooms has to contribute money. If you can't give the child money, the child won't pass the grade. It's really tough here: you don't pass if you don't have money. ❯

A second woman joined in:

> ❬ This is my son and he's finished 4th grade. He asked me for 12,000
> dong to give to the school. I borrowed 6,000 dong for him. He came
> back and said: 'I will not pass this year. The teacher said I will not pass,
> because I don't have the other 6,000 dong for the labour fund.' I told
> him: 'If that's what the teacher said, stay at home. I don't have 6,000
> dong to give you. Father is sick and I don't have money — everybody's
> asking for money.'
>
> I agree that kids have to learn and to work, and that's OK if it's only
> once a week or once a month. The school has been built, so the kids
> should at least have to work less. They are so small and they have to dig
> out grass. When the teachers do their groundnuts, the kids have to carry
> dung for their crop.
>
> About firewood: the teachers have their salary and they have Sunday
> as a holiday. So they should go to collect firewood themselves, or they should
> buy it from their salary. ... My kids said the teachers did not only stop
> them passing the grade, but they also locked them inside the classroom. ❭

A third woman added:

> ❬ ... The kids at this age should only eat, play, and learn, but they make
> them work, carry firewood. They are too small and they have to carry it a
> long way. The teachers shout at them when they are late. The kids are
> small, weak. They should rest on the way. It's cruel. It's excessive. ❭

In the house of the village headman, Mr Linh, the following day in Minh Quy,
villagers arranged a big meeting, to view the tapes from the other villages and
to record their own evidence. People talked even more vehemently about the
school, confirming the original claims against the teachers. They spoke about
the 'crimes' against the children and the 'dynasty' established by the
headmaster, his wife, and his daughter. The parents mentioned that they had
attempted to speak out at a school meeting once before, but that as a result their
children had been blacklisted by the teachers. One woman protested:

> ❬ ... We have complained at school/parents meetings, but the teachers
> do not change or learn any lessons. ... My kids dropped out. I should have
> persuaded them to go to school. ... The parents think they cannot afford
> for them to go and they drop out forever. ... When we spoke out in the school/
> parents meeting, the school management board blacklisted my kids.
> They threatened my kids: 'Your parents talked in a mess at a meeting.' ❭

A man alleged:

> ❮ After each meeting there is a protocol, but the headmaster never
> follows it. He just wants to turn the school into his 'dynasty'. Even the
> People's Committee made comments to the school, but they (the
> teachers) have never corrected their mistakes. The headmaster should
> bear the responsibility and should be competent to manage the school.
> They never implement any protocol. ❯

This session took several hours. Women, men, and even children spoke. As
the sun grew hotter, they crowded into the shade of Mr Linh's house. There
were pauses for translation, so that the non-Vietnamese members of the team
could understand; these pauses were always suggested by villagers. The
shared consultations of the 'evening cinema' sessions had established a
culture of collaboration. Huong's all-woman team of three nationalities,
working closely together to facilitate the work, and record sound and pictures,
seemed to enhance this feeling of trust and openness.

The time allotted to the pilot project was running out, so Huong asked
whether people would be prepared to view and check what had been recorded,
right away, and to let the Team know what they wanted included or excluded.
The whole group moved to a cooler garden location by Mr Linh's well to watch
the play-back and give their views. Three older women performed a little dance
in expression of their pleasure at hearing their families speak out.

Then Huong asked the villagers if they could make one or two positive
suggestions for solutions to the school problem. The villagers asked to show
the tapes from all three villages to the headmaster and the teachers and to ask
him, the Commune Committee, and the District for clarifications and
explanations. One mother said:

> ❮ ... We ask the film crew to let the Education Department know to stop
> teachers from exploiting the children's labour. The kids are forced to
> buy books from the headmaster's wife's shop. They told us the books
> from Quang Binh are not suitable. ❯

A second mother added:

> ❮ They are all printed in one Government Publishing House ... ❯

As part of the effort to cross-check the parents' allegations, it was decided that
Huong should visit the District Education Department in Ky Anh to find out
more about the labour policy for children in primary schools. She found the

Education Officers very open to discussion, so much so that she decided to describe the work of her team. The officers were enthusiastic and commented, 'People would never let us know or talk to us about such problems'.

Huong and Cuong also spent time discussing the whole process with the headmaster. They remained sensitive to the need for equity in the process of representation. They kept in regular contact, and were open with him about the accusations being levelled against him, his staff, and his family. He made a further recording, representing his views for presentation at the meeting planned by the villagers to take place with the Commune Committee, once they had approved the edited versions of the village tapes.

The main thrust of the headmaster's second tape, which was left unedited in its forty-minute version, was that the parents' anger resulted from misunderstanding and poor communication. He gave details of the labour rules and the school funds, and explained that he understood that the parents were poor, but that he kept both the requirements for children's labour and requests for funds for the school to a minimum.

> ◀ **Huong:** People complained about the labour fund. Could you explain what it is?
>
> **Headmaster:** We collect this fund every year, and it is not a labour fund. The fund is for school's expenses such as guests, payment for carpenters, etc. The people misunderstand. If they paid the labour fund, then labour (the labouring work done by the children) could be waived. It is not the case.
>
> **Huong:** People complained about the teachers threatening their kids, that they would not let them pass grade if they did not pay for the fund. Could you clarify this?
>
> **Headmaster:** The amount is decided at the beginning of the school year, but we collect the money at the harvest-time only. But some kids will not pay until they hear that they have passed the grade. So the teacher had to threaten them. For us teachers to have pupils that do not pass grade is very painful.
>
> **Huong:** People complained about different kinds of contributions. Could you clarify what they are?
>
> **Headmaster:** There are only a few kinds: the insurance for the pupils' benefit, and 200d for Cuba, which was the decision from the Politburo. At the end of last schooling year, we were so short of money and decided

to collect 2,000d from each child to cover the end-of-year ceremony, rewards ... etc. The contribution at the beginning of the year is 10,000d, for example, but we cannot collect it all at once. If the kids have 500d, we accept 500d; if they have 1000d or 2000d, we also accept it. ❯

He promised to come in person to meet the parents and the Commune Committee the following evening.

Conclusions (from the perspective of the trainer)

Villages are complex social structures. The question of the relationship between the micro-world of the village and the wider world of the District and Party authorities, beyond their own Commune People's Committee, had been introduced by the villagers themselves at the meeting at Mr Linh's house. They had also recognised the risks of speaking out, of naming the 'other camp' in the public sphere. By taking these steps, they had begun to analyse the structure of their problem and to look for resolution. The danger was that they might feel that Oxfam could protect them from later victimisation, while in fact the staff probably would not be able to do so. However, the greatest risk, as the parents had expressed it, was to their children's access to education.

Follow-up, and especially the maintenance of transparency in communication, would be crucial. The headmaster had previously been unwilling to meet the parents face to face, although he promised to attend the villagers' show-back to the Commune People's Committee, scheduled for the next evening. He had begun to reconsider his arguments, and his second tape gives a more serious response to the parents' complaints than the first.

For now, the videos from the three groups remained part of the same process, and in the next chapter we will follow the representation made by the villagers to the Commune People's Committee and to the District Authorities, using all the tapes produced in the Commune so far. We will follow the pilot project through to its formal 'end'. Nevertheless the 'end' of a project can never be quite so neat. While the outsiders may depart, the insiders remain. As we have noted, there are degrees of outsider-ness and insider-ness. The Vietnamese members of the Pilot team, as Oxfam project officers, had a different and longer-term relationship with the District, the Commune, and the villagers than did the rest of the pilot-project team, and this was understood by all the players.

The final evening of the Team's stay in Ky Nam was spent in planning with the villagers, the Commune People's Committee, and the school staff how the process would continue. This process of re-presentation will be discussed in the next chapter.

The role of the facilitator in PRA

Although the role of the facilitator is much discussed in relation to PRA,[1] the possibility of inconsistencies, and the overall effect on the information gained, as well as on the ownership of the information, is largely overlooked in the literature to date.

The key to local groups' perception of their own ability to act is their appropriation of their own learning. The facilitator should enable this to take place. Negotiation is crucial: not only to decide on the matters or agendas for research, but also on the activities that will be used to elicit information. Both these negotiations require facilitators to introduce themselves and their own roles with transparency. At the same time, both negotiations require a relationship of rapport and trust between facilitators and those with whom they wish to work.

Chambers describes one problem inherent in establishing such rapport: 'A problem is that capability depends on personality. Some people have a facility for using the "right" language, especially at international conferences, but behave in the "wrong" manner in the field, dominating, lecturing, interfering, interrupting and holding on to the stick.'[2] He emphasises that the 'magic' ingredient of 'good PRA' is facilitation, to make, and to enable the community to make and test, connections and cross-references that arise from the activities. But he says less about the cultural biases encoded in the activities themselves, and the need, therefore, to negotiate them.

Understanding and being able to reflect on these subtleties, in addition to being able to 'hand over the stick', defines the role and skill of the facilitator. The ability to plan and design research activities in an accessible and culturally relevant way implies, as Chambers indicates, the ability to appreciate the other's 'point of view' — in the sense of opinion, but also in the sense of culture and context. It is in the ability to assimilate this information and to act with it that facilitation of participatory research is framed.

Agreeing the agenda of the participatory research is in itself not enough: the purpose behind the research also has to be supported by a consensus which, in turn, will reflect two important considerations from the perspective of the local group: judgements about the intentions and veracity of the facilitators; and a perceived need for the research activities.

In Ky Nam visits from Oxfam staff are not at present a daily occurrence. What is more, as representatives of an international NGO, their arrival inevitably brings with it speculation about grant aid and improvements to material welfare. The negotiation of research agendas is affected by these considerations. And, as we shall see in the following chapter, they affect not only the attitudes of the participating community, but also the attitudes of the facilitators.

It is the development of a consciousness of the different identity and roles of facilitators that is inevitably most difficult to effect in a short-term training session. We can see the importance of transparency in the initial communications between a visiting team and the participating communities, and the effect of this on the expectations and choices that determine the community's ability critically to select appropriate agendas for research; but the immediate recognition of real practical or social problems should not be allowed to mask the prevailing cultural and political conditions.

While this training workshop in Ky Nam was a relatively short-term and one-off event, the sustainable learning for the communities lies in their own ability to progress through the experience, and to make use in the future of their learning about the relationships between the incomers and themselves, and about the processes of discussion, sharing, and representation. Knowledge produced by the exchange of information on the part of the local groups should be 'owned' by the villagers. This indicates the crucial importance of transparency in the introductory negotiations with the participants, which will affect choices about who participates.

Re-presentation and advocacy

5

Participatory representation and re-presentation

Participatory representation as a basis for communication should be seen as a continuum between the various players involved.

The word 'representation' can mean 'an image or likeness' of something; it can also mean 'acting or speaking on behalf' of someone. Participation in the creation of representative texts indicates the possibility of a synthesis of these two meanings. But such a synthesis demands constant renewal and revision. As with forms of political representation, the participation of a group in the production of an audio-visual text represents a particular moment, and this representation is not permanent. As with the delegation of the power to make political decisions, the mandate should be responsive and available for recall, affirmation, or renewal. The recorded moment represents a set of conditions in a context and at a point in time that has passed. The recording is already a secondary version that has been agreed as representative. The real context is fluid and changing, and may even change as a result of responses in other contexts to the video recording or programme itself. In this sense the representation offered by even the most participatory recording or programme is essentially temporary and requires regular renewal.

Village editorials

A very large proportion of the Ky Nam community attended the editorial discussion of the rough edits of the tapes produced so far. Women, men, and children from all three villages met after dark with the pilot-project teams in a garden of one of the houses in Minh Duc. Adults organised children to sit on the ground. The team had set up the TV monitor on the wall of the veranda. Binh and I.V. were busy starting the small generator, as far away in the dark garden as the cables would allow, so that the noise would not drown the video sounds. People were fetching benches from the surrounding houses, and there was a general buzz of excitement. Duongdi and Viengmone were setting up a camera, and Haida was organising a microphone to record the discussion after the tapes had been shown. The two small video lights would be used on batteries to supply light for the recording.

When everyone was settled — probably over one hundred people, although it was difficult to count heads by the light of the moon — the parents warned their children to keep the noise down, so that everyone could hear, and the showing began. Four tapes had been made:

- **Minh Duc** — *The Sea Dyke*: a report on the problems of sea-water flooding, and villagers' suggested solutions.
- **Minh Quy** — *Earth and Water*: a report on the problems of irrigation, water-storage, and income-generation.
- The two *Education* tapes: the parents' discussions about the corruption at the only primary school available to their children, and the headmaster's reply.

The three trainee teams had worked in rotation through the night to put together a version of each of the tapes, using the method of copying from the camera to the domestic video recorder.

The **Minh Quy** tape now included a section about women and income-generation, which had resulted from the point raised by women during the earlier play-backs. There were two interviews with women. In the first, a woman swings in a hammock and describes her typical day. She talks about her family and her loan from the State agricultural bank, which she used to buy a cow. She says she is not likely to take out another loan, because just thinking about the repayment of her current loan keeps her awake at night. The second interview is with a mother bringing up five children on her own. She says she manages to live by making rice wine, and recycling the waste to feed her pigs:

> ❜ I borrow one million from the bank with interest of 0.2 per cent per month, and I will have to pay back after three years. I make alcohol and use the waste to feed my pigs. It's quite easy to make alcohol, because the brewer's yeast is available in the market. ❜

The team had asked her about her hopes for the future, and her reply reflected the two urgent aspirations that had been voiced by villagers throughout the past ten days:

> ❜ for my children to be able to go to school, and enough water for the rice crop ❜

The **Minh Duc** tape had developed outwards from the initial problem of the sea-water flooding and the model showing the village solution and the angled sea dyke; it now included the locations and explanations put forward by the villagers. They showed how aquaculture and fishing could work to solve their economic problems, and how the salination had affected their rice fields. The programme is poetic (beginning and ending with the poems of the old farmer), but it is also scientific and informative.

The *Education* group had edited together the complaints of the parents from the three villages. Their tape ends with the parents' suggestions for solutions. The headmaster's replies were left unedited. It was felt that his right to reply should not be curtailed by anyone other than himself, and there had been no time to consult him or to facilitate his participation in an editing process.

The editing of the tapes was approved by the villagers. Among many comments made, one person said: 'You know, we live in such poverty and hardship that it is only now, watching the video, we realise how beautiful our place is.'

Following the editorial play-back there was a lively discussion about the local, national, and international uses of the tapes. The villagers said they should show the tapes to the District authorities. It was clear that the villagers who had worked on the *Sea Dyke* tape in Minh Duc, and those from Minh Quy who had worked on *Earth and Water*, had high hopes that their advocacy would be heard and seen not only by the District authorities but also by international funders. One man, who had worked on *Sea Dyke*, said:

> ❮ The people here are looking forward to receiving support from the central government and the local authorities, and from the other international humanitarian organisations. ❯

The villagers spent some time discussing and organising the show-back for the Commune Committee, already planned for the next evening (the penultimate day of the pilot project). It was agreed that this should take place on neutral ground at the Guest House. Perhaps the decision to hold it there reflected some nervousness about the probable reception of the specifically critical material about the primary school.

Working towards transparency — with local media

During the afternoon of the penultimate day, the three teams ran a workshop for the local Ky Anh TV broadcasting station staff about the whole process in Ky Nam, as it had so far developed. The Oxfam Country Representative in Vietnam had foreseen from the outset that the small team at the local station might be involved in the introduction to the participatory uses of video, and the trainer had already spent a day with the station team.

The role of the Ky Anh District broadcasting station is to relay short news stories from the district to VTV in Hanoi. These reports mainly consist of commune and district meetings and events. The material is generally filmed mute, and a voice-over is dubbed during editing. The reason for this approach stems partly from a Soviet film tradition of documentary-making, in which some of the staff were trained, and also, presumably, from the control that such an approach imposes on the messages conveyed. But there is also a material and practical reason: the lack of a suitable portable microphone. At present there is no way that sound can be collected live outside the small regional TV offices.

The contact between the pilot project and the local broadcasters was seen as an important contribution to creating good relations and transparency between government-run mass media and the participatory work that was being piloted in this project.

The local broadcasting team was intrigued by both the technical and participatory approaches taken in Ky Nam. As film-makers they found the location recording of high-quality sound appealing, as was the notion of using video recordings as a process of research and problem-solving with the villagers. As government employees, working under the strict surveillance of the National Broadcasting remit, they were also perhaps concerned about the freedom of speech and contentious debate that such a process produced.

Representation and re-presentation by villagers to the Commune People's Committee

That evening, from 7.30 to past midnight, representatives from the three villages showed their tapes to the Commune People's Committee. Unfortunately the headmaster was sick. This appeared to be a genuine illness: when Huong went to visit him to report back the following day, he was still ill. The meeting was packed by women, men, and children from the three villages. All four tapes — the two education tapes, and the tapes from Minh Duc and Minh Quy — were shown. The workshop teams and the guest-house staff, many of whom originated from the villages and were by now deeply involved with the progress of the pilot project, struggled through the night with an electric storm, a damp generator, and steamy 100 per cent humidity.

The Oxfam team members facilitated a discussion which divided the issues raised into problems that could be solved by the villagers themselves (for example cleaning out the reservoir) and those which would require external help (building up the reservoir walls and completing the irrigation canals). The filmed discussions took place after each tape had been viewed. There were many speakers from the People's Committee, mostly very poorly dressed and some quite elderly. It seemed that the People's representatives in Ky Nam were little better off than their constituents. The trappings of power were difficult to discern in any material form.

The teams shared the filming and recording. As the night progressed, a fan was improvised from a large sheet of cardboard to wave on the backs of the sweating camera team.

The outsiders had thought that the villagers and the Commune Committee might have been bored watching the headmaster's 40-minute reply to the parents' complaints, but they insisted on watching it all. After a long discussion, the meeting decided that both headmaster and parents had right on their side, but that they had not previously communicated and that this had led to a lot of misunderstandings. The meeting felt that there should be further discussions between the villagers, the Commune authorities, and the teachers, to draw up some ground rules and agreements about contributions of cash and labour, and future means of communication. They asked for the help of the Oxfam staff in organising a meeting to start this process before the beginning of the September term.

Meanwhile the meeting agreed that representatives from each village should take up an invitation which had been extended by the Chairman of the District to go to Ky Anh next morning to show all four tapes. The meeting finally broke up at around one in the morning.

Re-presentation to the Chairman of the District

Three villagers — Mr Linh, Mr Tho, and Mrs Them, one from each village — accompanied the pilot-project teams to the District offices in Ky Anh the next morning. They were greeted by the District Chairman and sat with him at the polished table of the main committee room. After watching all four tapes, he made the following observations.

On the Minh Duc Sea Dyke tape:

> ❦ It is very good to hear the voices of the people. It clarifies issues for the District to hear their local knowledge of the 'science' of their own area. It shows us clearly what the District can do, and what others higher up should be doing. Most importantly, it shows how conscious the people are of their own needs and the causes of their problems.
>
> The villagers' findings are right and are confirmed by the report from the Hanoi Water Resources University. There is also a need to replace the trees at the river-mouth. ❧

On the Minh Quy tape about the reservoir and irrigation:

> ❦ I find in the tape people speak out very clearly about their needs and
> their problems. It is quite clear that the first concern is water and then
> income-generation, besides rice, aquaculture, and other crops. ... There
> are four important considerations:
>
> 1 to improve the irrigation system;
> 2 reafforestation to protect the watershed;
> 3 capital for production;
> 4 knowledge about new income-generation methods.
>
> I can see from the proposals on the tape that some things people can do them-
> selves, and some things people need help with. It is a very valuable film to
> show, with the other film about the sea dyke, to people in other communes. ❧

On whole production of the workshop, after seeing the two Education tapes:

> ❦ I am really moved. For Ky Nam Commune it is the first time they
> have had such valuable tapes.
>
> I think this way of making film is very useful for raising community
> education. It is the people themselves who educate themselves. And this
> is a very lively and fresh form of documentation and has important
> implications for management. The District will need to re-examine its
> way of management of communes, because this participation boosts
> the villagers' way of thinking.
>
> I would like to talk about the content and use of these tapes. Besides
> the objective to show the wishes, voices and desires of the people, I'd like
> the tapes to be used in different districts and communities. I'd like the
> first two films especially to be shown to all Ky Anh people. ❧

At this stage, the pilot-project teams and the village representatives were in a
state of some anxiety about how the Chairman would respond to the education
tapes and the parents' criticism of the school. He went on:

> ❦ It's no shame to talk about our problems, and it's the only way to
> find solutions. I was informed by Huong that this film is to be continued
> in September. So I would propose that it is not shown very widely until
> then. I would like to propose that you come to work again with the
> Commune and the headmaster to find solutions to your problems and
> to find the way to make the people and the school closer and closer, so
> that the gap between the people and school is gradually closed and
> misunderstandings are resolved.

> The issue of transparency should be addressed by the headmaster in front of the parents' meeting, and the expenditure should be explained for next year, and there should be careful monitoring of expenditure during the year, so our film will make the parents, school, children, and community closer ... 〕

It was clear from this statement that Mr Tran had endorsed the process used in Ky Nam, but that he wanted to see the education issue followed through to some kind of conclusion.

After a pleasant lunch with the Chairman in the District office's restaurant, the pilot team and the village representatives returned to Ky Nam. The three village representatives asked the Oxfam Project Officers to organise a meeting that evening with the Commune Committee, parents, and teachers to ensure that a date was agreed for a public meeting to discuss setting up a parent-teachers' association and an open-book accounting system. They were determined that all the local parties should agree a date for this meeting and set it up with the District Education Authority before the beginning of the new school year in September.

Concerns for representation and communication in the future

This was the last day of fieldwork and the sun was already going down. The teams went to fetch people from the villages in the project cars. A member of the Education team later recorded in the group diary:

> 〔 Minh Duc and Minh Tien people did not want to come, because it was late and they had to guard their houses and kids (or they are afraid, because they have been threatened by the Commune?) Note: I did not see any light in any of the houses I went to. The head of the Commune Party came and some other representatives. The headmaster, his wife, and three other women teachers came. Only two or three parents who spoke out in the film came. 〕

The meeting took place in the dark garden of a neighbouring rest house, under the trees, with small candle lamps on low tables, and the sound of the sea in the distance. The group gathered around the tables included the headmaster and his wife, four or five teachers, the Chairman of the People's Committee and several committee members, and a small group of villagers. Only the Oxfam members of the pilot team sat with this group, as it was they who would participate in and record the public meeting in September. The rest of the team sat a little back and listened to the proceedings with our interpreter. Huong opened the meeting:

❦ This meeting has not been called to reach any conclusions, because not everyone could be represented here. But at the beginning of the next school year there should be a bigger meeting attended by everyone. That meeting is being organised to take place on 20 September, and this time it is hoped all the parents will attend. [There was a general murmur of agreement.] The original films will be shown back again then. ❞

Cuong and Huong went on to emphasise that the films had simply been a way of enabling the villagers to collect their thoughts and represent their concerns.

After speeches from several teachers and the villagers present, in which they rehearsed many of their earlier arguments, the Chairman of the People's Committee of the Commune summarised the agreement to call the meeting of parents, teachers, and the Education Authority for 20 September, and he invited the Oxfam project team to return to record the proceedings. He concluded by saying that throughout the pilot project he had been impressed by 'the openness, respect and caring for people that had been shown by the visitors'.

On reflection, the team still had some concerns about this meeting: that it had been too rushed, and that the villagers had not turned out because it was called at the last minute, and followed the exhausting meeting the night before. They also felt that they should have made it possible for the villagers to introduce the whole evening, so that the teachers and Commune would not have found it so easy to dominate the proceedings. The outcome would not be clear until the September reunion.

Trainee learning reviewed

The team left for Hanoi early next morning. In effect, it was too soon for the project as a whole to be evaluated. The results of a more long-term evaluation of the outcomes in the villages, and for Oxfam UK and Ireland institutionally, will be discussed in Chapter 6.

At this stage, in the tired but rather elated moment of winding up the workshop on our return to Hanoi, it would have been inappropriate to proceed any further with the evaluation of the project than a preliminary consideration (see Table 7) of the various aspects of learning that the project had indicated.

Reflections about training and representation

Learning about representation seemed, at this stage of the project, to be less problematic than it appeared one year later. At this stage, it seemed that, within the limits of the time available, and the complicated issues that had arisen in Ky Nam,

Table 7: Outcomes discussed in Hanoi in a brief evaluation of the workshop

Villagers' learning	Pilot-project team's learning	Institutional learning
• Using video to construct arguments, retrieve information, and find solutions • Working with and influencing outsiders • Using video to listen to each other in a situation of conflict and to find ways of resolving conflict • Using video to represent themselves individually and in groups	• Basic video production skills • Basic participatory learning approaches • Facilitation skills • Sharing and mutual support • Maximising skills within the team • Transparency with all partners • Involving villager participants in team learning and sharing • Using video to collect, cross-refer, and retrieve facts and opinions • Keeping participants in step with all available information • Making it fun, both for the participants and for the team members	• Video is not expensive, time-consuming, or fraught with difficulty.[1] • Beneficiaries can speak/ have ideas about their own needs, conflicts, and situations. • Video processes can help them to hear each other and to be heard. • Participatory video production, unlike standard development videos, gives the community control of taped material, and control over the way in which they are represented. • By combining video with participatory learning methods, communities can retrieve and discuss their own needs and decide what, and how, they want to communicate to others.

the teams had succeeded in enabling the villagers in all three villages to participate in setting their own agendas and representing the problems they had identified.

In their brief review of the training in Hanoi, the team members all valued the experience they had gained of working together and critically reviewing their own progress. They felt that the team process had ensured that all the trainees were able to participate in all aspects of the work, and that the skills of the whole group were well represented and shared.

They felt that this sharing and the opportunities to review the processes critically had particularly helped them to maintain equity in the matter of the primary-school conflict.

The relationships within the team had been reflected in the relations between the teams and the villagers, and this was indicated in the villagers' participation, after the first few days, in the discussions at the evening 'cinema'.

The team had enabled all three villages to re-present their views at all stages, to the school, the Commune, the Education authorities, and the District authorities. Furthermore, the village representatives at these meetings had reported back. It was felt at the Hanoi review that it was clear to the villagers that, in the case of the school conflict, their presence would be included in the future representation at the meeting set up for September.

The question of the identity of the key participants in each editorial group had been less clearly addressed. While in Minh Quy, the team was aware of the very constant presence of the village headman, Mr Linh, who was also a member of the Commune Committee. His role at various moments of the process was less transparent. He had been organising and possibly selecting village contacts in the early stages, but by the time of the meeting of parents at his house in the later stages of the discussions about the primary school, his control was much less obvious. Many women had spoken and in fact led the discussions about education in all three villages, and again at the meeting at Mr Linh's house. However, it was he who represented Minh Duc in the meeting with the District Chairman.

Likewise, the initial contact of the team in Minh Duc had been with the Head of the Women's Union, who was also a member of the Commune People's Committee. It would have been interesting to know how much influence she had in selecting other key participants. Yet once the technical discussions about the design of the sea dyke got under way, it was almost inevitably a group of men who had taken the principal roles.

Typhoons and evaluations

6

In the light of the objectives outlined in the original proposal, the pilot project in Vietnam should be evaluated at many different levels:

- village learning and the practice of representation;
- local Party and authority learning about villagers' participation and representation;
- institutional learning at the level of Oxfam in Vietnam, in the UK and Ireland, and in the regional Oxfam offices around the world;
- Oxfam supporters' learning about village life, needs, and capacities in Vietnam.

In other words, while the project has implications for the participation and learning of village people, conclusions can also be drawn for Oxfam's institutional learning, including its own relationships with governments and donors. As some of the village material was also to be used with Oxfam supporters in the UK, it must be approached from the angle of institutional learning and the learning among Oxfam's supporters about the specific nature of participation in a given socio-political and cultural context. In the shorter term, evaluation of the pilot project should also address the outputs, the tapes themselves, and any tangible changes they provoked.

To quote the original brief for the pilot-project proposal:

> Ultimately this initiative must be assessed by whether it has contributed towards bringing about sustainable changes to poor people's lives, and this must be centrally informed by their values and priorities. Projects cannot be deemed 'successful' or 'failures' if the perceptions of the beneficiaries diverge seriously from those of the 'objective' external evaluator.
>
> It is suggested that local Oxfam staff, beneficiaries, and those in Oxfam House are asked to assess the effectiveness of video against the above objectives in terms of their different needs and their assessment of performance. As Riddell (1990) suggests in terms of evaluation methods: '*In short, it is unnecessary to concentrate time, effort and resources on project or programme evaluation if firm conclusions can be drawn without*

using sophisticated techniques. Similarly, if judgements made about qualitative aspects of projects are not substantially challenged by the relative 'actors' or groups ... then purist worries about objectively assessing these factors become largely irrelevant. The results should then constitute the basis for different stakeholders to assess to what degree such techniques and methods fulfil their different information needs.'[1]

In looking for ways of presenting an evaluation of this project from the various perspectives outlined, it was decided that one or two of the original Vietnamese team would revisit Ky Anh and Ky Nam one year later. In the event, only Huong was available to go on the evaluation visit; her report will be included here.

In fact, she visited Ky Anh more than once during the period between the pilot project in July 1995 and the evaluation in September 1996. Both these visits offer interesting reflections on the perspectives of villagers and trainees about the teaching and learning which took place during the field workshop.

Huong was accompanied by Binh and Cuong during her first follow-up visit, in September 1995. This was for the meeting between the Commune authorities in Ky Nam, the Education Department for the District of Ky Anh, and the parents of the primary-school children in Ky Nam. The meeting, held in the Commune headquarters building in the village, was very well attended and was filmed by Huong, Cuong, and Binh (now known collectively as the Oxfam Vietnam Grassroots Video Team). Huong's diary of the visit includes details of the preparation for the meeting with the various players.

◀ *18 September 1995*
I went with Binh to the three villages and talked with people who spoke out in the education tapes. The main feedback was that the headmaster's wife had threatened people who passed her shop (on Highway One). She threatened that people who had spoken in the film would be listed and 'dealt with'. Some women said that their husbands had shouted at them for speaking out. But everyone was enthusiastic about the meeting on the 20th.

We went to the Commune and handed them the two tapes (the parents' and the headmaster's tapes) and asked about the meeting. They said that it would take place as planned (at the pilot project's final evening in July).

Then we went to the school and met the headmaster and the other teachers. They all asked to see the film again. We arranged to show it to them on the night of 19th September.

At 4pm, as planned the day before, Mr Truc, Mr Vinh, and Mr Nhuan from the District Education Department came to our place. We showed them the tapes. There was some discussion. Then they said that it is their problem. They want to solve it, because Oxfam is not going to be here for ever. Oxfam comes and goes. We appreciated that and said that we were very happy for them to handle the meeting. Then they suggested postponing it. We insisted, saying: 'Even though we are outsiders, we still want to witness it while we are here.' They agreed with us and also agreed to our suggestions of ground rules. And they offered their guarantee that nothing bad would happen to the children and the parents who spoke out. They also agreed that Mr Truc and Mr Vinh will come to the school and the Commune to discuss the agenda for the meeting.

19 September

7.30 pm. We put on a show-back for all the teachers, the head of the District Education Department, and the head of the Commune Party. Mr Truc made an opening statement. We (the Oxfam team) repeated again the ground rules, and they all agreed. The headmaster's wife laughed from beginning to end, indicating that she did not take the video seriously, but the other teachers looked more serious. They watched both tapes. Some teachers claimed that the parents had said unfair things to them. The head of the Education Department said: 'We should feel thankful to those who spoke. They criticised us because they love us. They would not criticise otherwise. Those who threatened the parents I would not consider as teachers.' [Huong comments that, according to Ho Chi Minh's philosophy, Party officials should be the servants of the people.]

20 September

The meeting was held in the Commune meeting house and chaired by Mr Linh, the head of the Parents' Committee. (The same Mr Linh who is the village headman in Minh Quy, and who represented his village at the show-back for the Chairman of the District on the last day of the pilot project.) A lot of people came (about 200 parents), and more men than women. A lot of people had to sit outside. We were worried that we were going to see some kind of set-piece drama. But we calmed down as soon as the meeting started. People began to criticise the Commune People's Committee for not providing enough chairs and space for the parents, even though they knew about the meeting two months ago. They pointed out that those sitting and those standing would not have the same rights when speaking. 'Why do you, the headmaster, and you, the Head of the People's Committee, occupy a chair each?', they asked. 'Bring in more chairs and reorganise the whole room so that everyone can sit.' Binh, Cuong, and I now recognised that this Commune is really the homeland of Revolution.

The meeting went very well. We videoed 120 minutes. People spoke more calmly and reasonably. They criticised the school, but also themselves. The parents proposed that the school should have a communications book and that a Communications Committee between the school and the parents should be formed.

A parent speaker: 'Parents have already said lots of things. Now we must strike at the cause and solution of our problems. We must decide which problems are the responsibility of the school and which are the responsibility of the family. ... We should discuss the level of our contributions. As Mr Duong has rightly said, there has been no accounting by the school. From now on there must be a contact book. Anything needed by the school must be written down by the teacher in the contact book for the parents' information. All contributions should be in cash. A brick [i.e. any material contribution such as wood or manure] is the equivalent of money. Let us contribute in cash.'

Mr Linh from the Education Department made a speech. The Education Department had to protect their teachers. Other parents raised issues about requests from the school that they should buy health insurance for their children, but that they were not offered certificates. And the headmaster spoke, confessing to the problems at the school.

Headmaster: 'The school has admitted faults and shortcomings. To overcome these, the parents have to elect a liaison board for contact with the school. Now I would like to explain something.

Firstly, the handing in of firewood by Grade 1. Grade 1 children are not supposed to cut wood, because they are very small. Grade 1 should only do light work, i.e. grass uprooting or flower growing. Any parents who see Grade 1 children chopping wood, please write to me directly.

Secondly, the issue of insurance. Mr Tuan has explained that when a child is injured, the school or the health centre must have a report. We cannot solve the matter without an initial report. You must write a report saying what time and what date it happened. There aren't any insurance cards for children yet. The card has to look like this and needs to be in pressed plastic. ... So anything related to insurance, please meet the school. Even if the accident took place on the mountain, the parents and school will write a report and I myself will sign it. Formalities are needed for this kind of thing.

Thirdly, the issue of the class of compassion [a class designated for the children of destitute families]. This class was formed during the time that Mr Din worked at the school — and he handed it over to me. I don't think that is a problem for our school. I would like, at this meeting, to ask that this class should be re-started. Any poverty-stricken child will be admitted to this class.' **"**

(Transcribed from the video recording of the 20 September 1995 meeting)

Huong's diary continues:

❝ After the public meeting we had a meeting with Mr Truc and Mr Vinh from the Education Department. They have a plan to form a Parent-Teacher Association in every school in the district in October and November. They want to show the tapes as an example [of how parents and teachers can be brought together]. They also plan to show the film at the Headmasters' Conference and the Education Conference for the whole District. **❞**

Her diary for the visit ends with the comment:

❝ We can witness here that in other places people are harvesting, but in Ky Nam the rice is only about 20 cm high and the fields do not look much greener than in July. **❞**

Reading Huong's diary in the UK a few days after her visit, I felt proud for the Oxfam Grassroots Video Team, that they had maintained equity of access for all the players in this conflict. And that as a result they had felt empowered to insist with the Education Department that the meeting should take place and that a video record should be made. It was also interesting that they had taken on board the lesson about setting ground rules, which we had discussed after what we felt had been our mistaken handling of the meeting on the final night of the pilot project, when we had planned the one on 20 September. We felt then that we had fallen into the trap of allowing one side — the teachers — to dominate the proceedings, by not first asking them to agree ground rules for equal time for representations from different factions.

Huong's evaluation visit to Ky Nam one year after the pilot project

A year later, between 11 and 14 September 1996, Huong visited Ky Nam again, with the specific task of making a follow-up evaluation of the whole pilot project from the point of view of the villagers, the Commune People's Committee, the headmaster and teachers of Ky Nam Primary School, Mr Truc, the Head of Ky Anh Education Department, Mr Tran, the Chairman of the District Committee, and Mr Din, the Head of the People's Council.

Huong writes that her visit was hard, because it took place in the middle of a typhoon, and she had to get away again before Highway One was flooded.

Outcome of the primary-school debate

Huong reports that all the people interviewed were very happy with progress at the school. After the meeting held in September 1995 between the school, the Commune authorities, and the Education Department, the school became much more transparent in making requests for contributions. Any contributions now had to be discussed and agreed by the Commune authorities. 'There are no more unreasonable contributions and unnecessary labour,' commented Mr Lu from Minh Quy. The business of forcing the children to bring in firewood and animal manure had stopped.

During the school year 1995–1996, the school held three Parent-Teacher meetings. The school sent teachers to villages to talk to parents about the value of education and to persuade them to send the drop-out children back to school. The communication between the community and the school was now very much better. The school had also sent teachers to talk to the Women's Union about how to raise awareness among mothers about nutrition and child health.

below Play-time at Ky Nam primary school.

Oxfam/Sean Sprague

The villagers clearly see the use of video in this case. As a woman from Minh Duc commented to Huong:

❧ We raised this problem many times before, but things did not change. Now facts are recorded on video and it's people's opinion and everybody can look at it, and the school no longer dares do the wrong things. They are made accountable, because they fear that outsiders may come and check.

At the school meetings [in the past], we would not dare to express our views so directly. Here it can be recorded on video and shown to others, and we are not afraid, because it is the truth. ❧

Huong writes:

❧ Video is seen as a tool to express one's opinion publicly and to keep people accountable for what they promised.

In the view of District Education Department, it was good to let people express opinions which might be right or wrong. The process brought progress, because it was handled very carefully, by the video team and also by the Education Department. It was a deep misunderstanding and miscommunication and it was painful for the people and for the teachers. The conflict was resolved in a tactful way which enabled people to express their opinions. The headmaster was able to reply in another tape, and this opened the way for the meeting (on 20 September 1995) where all the parties were able to clear up outstanding problems and define the direction for the future with good will.

The Education Department reported that they had shown the three tapes (the people's tape, the headmaster's tape and the meeting tape produced on 20 September) to the Headmasters' conference in October 1995. Many headmasters had felt able to admit that they have similar problems of miscommunication. They understood from the tapes the importance of keeping a transparent accounting system. In the opinion of the Education Department, it would have been wrong to show the film on Ky Anh Television, because there would not have been an opportunity to solve the problem and it would probably have escalated.

The Education Department see clearly the difference between the two types of video: the Oxfam type and the news type on television, which they described as 'very superficial'. They wanted to propose to Oxfam to approve a video camera and a video training for Education Department staff, so that they can themselves record interesting PTA meetings. They were especially keen to film the District Education conference in November 1996 and then to take the tapes to other schools/communes. They felt that the costs for doing this might come out of Oxfam's biodiversity campaign budget funded by a local embassy. **'**

Huong writes that she thinks it would be a good idea for local cadres to have training in participatory video skills, provided that the people chosen were sensitive, knowledgeable about development issues, and sure to use this tool carefully. She points out that identifying such cadres would not be easy.

'The Sea Dyke' and 'Earth and Water'

Huong's report also discusses the other two tapes made during the pilot project in 1995. She writes that people interviewed were unhappy, because 'they wanted a sea dyke and a reservoir, and they got a film'.

> **'** People interviewed pointed out that the villagers themselves, the Commune and the District Authorities all knew about the need for the sea dyke long before the video team came, but they did not have any funding.
>
> Nevertheless the video making had led to very high expectations, especially when villagers were asked their opinions for technical solutions, and they worked hard with the video team to explore these issues using models.
>
> In the District Authority's view, it was good to let people express their desire. Mr Tran pointed out that villagers want many things: sea dyke, aquaculture, reservoir and so on; this shows that people are active in thinking what to do best on their land. But they do not have money, experience, and techniques. He felt that it was good to enable them to discuss these things. But the process had raised their expectations and, if there is no follow-up, the film making will have negative impacts. He felt also that the process was costly in terms of the time it took. However, as a result of the film, some Commune cadres from Ky Nam were invited to attend the Hoang Dinh sea-dyke building-techniques workshop organised by the Ha Noi Water Resources University in November 1995.
>
> The District People's Committee showed the films for the staff of the People's Committee and People's Council at the Rural Development training workshop for them to see the real situation, and the wishes of the people. And the Party also showed the films to Misereor, a German NGO which was interested in the project and is trying to find funding for it.

The head of the Party sees the videos as valuable to show to donors. But he feels that they would be even more useful if they were accompanied by a detailed project proposal and technical drawings. **'**

Huong reports that Oxfam Vietnam had also been trying to get funding for the Ky Nam sea dyke. The film was shown to two British Members of Parliament who visited Ky Anh and Ky Nam. More recently (November/December 1996), Oxfam, the District, and the British government's Overseas Development Administration (now Department for International Development — DFID) held a logical-framework planning workshop to prioritise the infrastructural projects needed for the alleviation of poverty in the region. DFID is now planning to fund the Ky Nam sea dyke with a five-year grant, in response to pressure from Oxfam and the District, through the use of the video.

Issues about participation in the context of Vietnam

Huong's evaluation report discusses the participation of the villagers in the pilot project. She writes:

> **'** It was quite shocking to find out how many of the people who participated in the video-making process with us were assigned by their heads of villages. People from Minh Quy who participated in the *Earth and Water* film were assigned by Mr Linh, the head man of Minh Quy village. **'**

She reports that the participants were people who had more time and were better off, and more knowledgeable about the reservoir work. The women from Minh Duc, who were so vociferous in the *Education* tape, also said they were assigned by the village head man, because their houses were nearer to the road. Mrs Diep from Minh Duc told Huong:

> **'** Had we not have been assigned, we would not have participated, because it was so time-consuming, it was so hot, and we lost several days of work. **'**

A second woman from Minh Duc observed:

> **'** At the beginning, I was told there would be some payment, but there was nothing at the end. **'**

Mr Lu from Minh Quy, who took part in *Earth and Water*, commented:

> **'** I was honoured to be assigned by the Party and selected by the people. We were told to participate because there was a hope that Oxfam would

help for something and I was happy to be with the team for five days, even though my wife nagged me for wasting the time. Seeing myself on the screen, I felt very honoured and privileged. 〉

The general feeling was that people were assigned to participate, in the hope that Oxfam would fund the sea dyke or the reservoir. Huong writes:

〈 From the video team side, we wanted to see it as a participatory process for the villagers to share the problem and find the solution for it, to speak out with their own voices, and we hoped to see 'empowerment' of the people through this process. In my opinion, poor people know why they are poor and they know that they need a sea dyke to protect their livelihoods and their land. (They know they need) a proper irrigation system to provide enough water for their fields, and that it will make their life much better.

Everybody knows this, from the very poor farmer to the Commune and District authorities, but they do not have the money. If there is no sea dyke after such a video-making process, there will be frustration and disempowerment. People will lose their hope and trust. The video team wanted the people to own the film, but they do not. They still see the film as Oxfam's film.

The women in Minh Duc and people in Minh Quy participated more freely in the Education tapes, because they were so unhappy about the problem of the primary school. 〉

She records the comment of Mrs Diep from Minh Duc:

〈 We were nagged at after we had talked on the film by some of the teachers and commune authorities, but we did not fear, because we knew what we said was fact. 〉

Huong continues:

〈 The participation issue in video and in PRA, and in all of our work, raises similar problems, at least in the Vietnamese context. Participation in a communist environment is very different, because of the element of organised democracy. The form is there, but there is a vacuum of power relations between those in power, who think the people are not capable, and the people themselves. If you want to see the result of participation, it takes time and must be part of the whole cycle of participation, representation, re-presentation, negotiation, and practical experience. This has implications for the way that Oxfam sees participation in development and the manner in which development workers interact and consult with villagers. You have to establish accountable relations and to be the person from whom they can seek help and advice. **'**

The issue about who participated and how they were selected is of great concern, especially to the Vietnamese Oxfam staff, because they are anxious about the whole future of participatory approaches in the current climate in Vietnam. There are two distinct concerns:

- How can the poorest people in a village find a voice, if the authorities are selecting those who will participate?
- In a context of poverty, are people empowered through participation in problem-solving, if they are not able to achieve the solutions they have proposed?

The first of these concerns clearly addresses the definition of 'community' proposed by the Oxfam Vietnam Country Representative, in his briefing to the Pilot Team, when he spoke of the community as 'the people and government together'. His definition accepts the cultural and political context as it exists in Vietnam today. Both people and People's Committee are poor in Ky Nam. There are grades of poverty — but one could debate long and hard about these. The importance of the Representative's definition of community in the Vietnamese context is that it recognises the cultural and the political dimension of Vietnamese life. We can see from the old farmer's song (quoted in the Introduction) that these two elements are deeply fused in the Vietnamese context. And we can also see from the outspoken complaints by the parents about the way that the Party had organised the seating for the meeting on 20 September 1995, and their claims to equal rights of representation at that meeting, that the people recognise that they can challenge the Party, at least at the village level.

The issue of participation is complicated in this evaluation by the people's desire for representation of their needs. On the one hand, as Huong reports, everyone from the poorest farmer to the Commune and District leaders knows, for example, that Minh Duc needs a sea dyke. On the other hand, they are angry with her, as the Oxfam representative, because they had not been kept informed that representations were taking place and were in the process of bearing fruit. They had not been present at the various stages of negotiations to re-present their own demands. The processes of negotiation had remained invisible to them.

Mr Hong, the Vice-Chairman of the Commune Party Committee, said in reply to a question from Huong about future work in Ky Nam:

> ❦ Do not do anything until you do the sea dyke and reservoir as promised: people are tired of waiting and will not be enthusiastic. ❦

Values in reflective approaches to development

Yet Huong's findings from different stakeholders offer conflicting evidence about the *Sea Dyke, Earth and Water,* and *Education* tapes, and their values. There is uniformly positive evidence about the value of the *Education* tapes. However, the *Sea Dyke* and *Earth and Water* tapes are also being used within and beyond the villages to lobby for funding for the projects, to meet the needs they describe.

Huong's feeling is that in poor communities like Ky Nam, people have to struggle to get enough food to survive and do not have leisure-time to waste. People are more interested in tangible outputs of activities to improve the economic situation than in intangible values such as 'process of participation' and 'empowerment'. The economic situation should be improved to empower them first. But significantly, the showings to various potential funders — Misereor, Oxfam in Hanoi, DFID, and so on — have not involved those who participated in making the tapes. The village participants are not aware that these fund-raising efforts have been taking place, or at least they have not witnessed or experienced them. As far as they are concerned, their hard work has produced no result.

This is certainly a weakness in the follow-up to the pilot project. The pilot project was intended to enable poor people to practise representation and re-presentation, but in fact, in respect of their two advocacy tapes, *Sea Dyke* and *Earth and Water,* they have had the experience of sending a message but receiving no reply. It is hardly surprising that Huong, as a representative of Oxfam, was verbally attacked by the villagers who spent so much time making models and participating in the filming. As we have seen, the villagers are part of a culture that is historically revolutionary. They are prepared to speak out.

Their ambivalent reaction to their participation in *Sea Dyke* and *Earth and Water* is significantly different from their endorsement of their participation in the *Education* tapes. And there was a significant difference in the follow-up to these two processes. The participants in the *Education* tapes subsequently took part in a whole series of show-backs, when they saw and heard reactions to their representations. They were participants and witnesses in processes of re-presentation. The results that were achieved have also been documented, and can be retrieved if the situation demands it.

The question arises: had the participants in the making of the *Sea Dyke* and *Earth and Water* tapes also been involved in the processes of using them for fund-raising and lobbying, and had they been kept informed about progress, would they have felt so frustrated a year later? As the woman from Minh Duc said, referring to her participation in the production of the *Education* tapes, the process allowed her to move her private complaints into an open forum. Although this has also happened in the case of the other issues represented in *Sea Dyke* and *Earth and Water*, the participants have not seen it happen. Twelve months is not a long time for the business of fund-raising.

Huong says that there is a danger, if the topic of a video is a tangible project requiring resources, that it will raise the community's expectation of material help. She recommends that video can be used in the preparation of a funding programme, if resources are available (money and staff time). She says that, as a principle, participatory approaches, including video and PRA, should be introduced alongside a clear funding programme. Otherwise, she says, it will bring reverse effects. And she adds that if funding is available, but the funders do not agree with proposed projects, this should be communicated to the community.

The other question, then, is about why the video recording process was seen as providing crucial evidence in the case of the *Education* tapes, but was seen as less important in the case of *Sea Dyke* and *Earth and Water*. Would this be the case were the projects to go ahead? In the past, for example, there have been many criticisms of the lack of local consultation that characterises projects, such as the construction of the reservoir and the irrigation system, carried out by government departments and funded by international donors. Failure to involve local people has resulted, according to testimonies in *Earth and Water*, in poor designs: the reservoir is lower than the fields, and the irrigation canals do not reach the level of the fields. Moreover, villagers do not feel a sense of ownership or responsibility for such resources. As a result, the reservoir is not cleaned and, as the villagers point out in the film, there are places where good fresh water is simply running away into the sea, because no one has closed a sluice or dug a small diversionary channel. All this material would provide useful and replayable evidence, similar to that of the testimonies in the *Education* tapes, if the villagers were involved in the process of fund-raising and later in the development of the projects for water-storage and irrigation.

Finally, Oxfam's willingness and ability to evaluate this project one year later should also be noted. This evaluation is particularly valuable in terms of the agency's own learning about the participatory uses of video in Vietnam and in other regions. At a meeting of Policy and Research staff and staff on the Asia Regional Desk at Oxfam's headquarters in Oxford in April 1997, Huong's evaluation and my own comments were discussed, and the specific difficulties of working in a participatory way in the current context of Vietnam were pointed out by the Vietnam Country Representative. It was noted particularly that Oxfam's 'hands-on' operational engagement in development projects in Vietnam is not typical of the way in which the agency works in other countries. Elsewhere Oxfam channels funds primarily through local NGOs. The direct funding of projects by Oxfam in the Ky Anh District meant, as we have seen, that participation, and particularly participatory communication in relation to material needs, was seen to be related in this process to the demand for funds. The feeling of the Oxfam April 1997 meeting was, in retrospect, that the choice of Vietnam for a pilot project of this kind had ignored this specific (unusual for Oxfam) operational relationship with projects. Had the funding been passed through a local NGO on the ground, closer day-to-day contact with village people in the follow up would have been possible.

Oxfam's ability and willingness to evaluate its institutional role and profile in this project points to the value of transparency between the funder and the other players, including the consultant, the training teams, and the local and district groups.

The use of video in enabling groups to analyse conflicts and choices

The Ky Nam experience produces some interesting reflections on the ambiguities that can result from project culture and design. The issue of primary education revealed that villagers had already defined the school teachers as members of an oppositional camp, and this definition fuelled their energy to participate in the process of research and representation. The careful handling of the process by the *Education* video team enabled the villagers and the headmaster to transcend their anger, to reflect on the problems, and to produce proposals for solutions. The important aspect of this process was that the video team negotiated opportunities for both representation and response. Both sides spoke, and — crucially — both sides listened and responded again. After the show-back to the District Chairman, boundaries changed between the parents' and the teachers' camps. In contrast, in the work on the sea dyke and the reservoir, when communication ceased, new camps were formed. The village participants in *Sea Dyke* and *Earth and Water* now saw Oxfam Vietnam as the 'other' — withholding money and wasting their time.

It is interesting to speculate whether the result would have been the same had the village participants in the construction of these two tapes been involved in discussions about the feasibility of meeting their needs — even if their expectations had been disappointed. It is possible that Oxfam would still have been identified as the enemy camp. However, it is also possible that, in the process of participation in the discussions about funding, the villagers of Ky Nam would have seen themselves more clearly as part of a District economic plan, and this might have offered them other insights and choices — and new knowledge. Initial research in Ky Nam had shown that the villagers of Minh Duc were already being moved to Minh Tien by the Commune, as a result of the salination of their fields. The villagers knew that their fields were becoming less and less fertile. If the construction of a sea dyke was not feasible — or simply too expensive to be justified within the broad economy — this learning would have been important.

Conclusions

The project might be criticised for not ensuring that a wider range of villagers was represented, but it is not clear how, within the time available for the pilot project, the teams could have intervened more effectively to make this happen. The poverty of everyone, including quite clearly the members of the Commune Committee themselves, had the effect of masking many of the obvious indicators of power, other than that indicated by gender. Other indicators of status, as we have seen, related to culture and to politics. In this first use of participatory media in Vietnam, it may be judged wise not to have taken investigation of the political power structures in the villages any further. However, in meeting the objectives of the pilot project — to enable villagers to practise representation — some useful initial progress appears to have been made.

Several steps were taken to introduce the concepts of participatory processes and representation in the world beyond the village. The meeting between the villagers, the trainees, and the local broadcasters had been conceived as one way of making sure that the rationale behind the participatory uses of video was understood and shared with other local media interests. The meetings with the Party, Education, and District authorities were intended similarly to involve these other players in the processes of community development. But ultimately sustainability would depend on a continuing commitment to transparency and the maintenance of dialogue, and we were aware that there were risks of recrimination not only within the community, but from other authorities beyond the District itself.

However, one important aspect of transparency had been missed by both the trainer and trainees. It was, in retrospect, an obvious omission. The villagers involved in the representations about the sea dyke had recorded their hopes for international finance. It should have been obvious that they were making assumptions about the power of the outsiders as representatives of foreign funders. In this respect the identity of the visiting team had not been made clear. Oxfam's reputation in the District had been instrumental in gaining permission to use video and to hold the training course there, and Oxfam's name and reputation had been used later in introductions to the villagers, as a way of legitimising our presence. However, in the villagers' vocabulary, the name 'Oxfam' meant money. Transparency would have required us as outsiders to demonstrate, from the beginning, that the power to allocate funds was not vested in our group. It would have required a clearer explanation to the villagers that they were invited to participate in the process of research-ing and structuring the subjects which they chose for the tapes, and that they would then be able to use them for their own purposes. Such a response would have included planning for future participation by the villagers, using the tapes for re-presentation, in the same way that those involved in the Education tapes had been involved in the planning of future meetings.

Transparency about the need to look for funding beyond Oxfam, and about the processes of re-presentation that this would involve, together with the possibilities of failure, would have led to learning opportunities for the villagers. They would have learned about the strategies and competition involved in fund-raising, and about the need to develop strategies for the future if needs are not met; they would also have gained a greater understanding of the relationship between international funders and local authorities.

The case-study in Ky Nam reveals the desire of villagers to use the medium of video to address or to practise addressing groups able to exercise power beyond their own contexts. They made it clear that they valued the opportunity to make a retrievable record of their own debates and meetings. The case-study also confirms the need to see representation and re-presentation from the point of view of the participating local groups, as progressive learning and renewable processes. This is clearly a shortcoming of projects which do not permit a long-term involvement with the local groups concerned. The limitations of fieldwork training in such cases need to be reviewed and understood by all the participants.

Field-work experience is crucial for understanding the complex issues arising from participatory representation and re-presentation. The experience of this case-study emphasises the need for transparency between trainers and the community hosts of field-work training. And there are indications of the need for comparative studies to inform future practice.

Outcomes of the pilot project in the participant agencies

Following the pilot project, the staff of Oxfam UK and Ireland in Vietnam have drawn up a video strategy document, aiming to integrate video work into all their grassroots development projects. Oxfam has sponsored several video-based activities since the pilot project:

- A film made by Cuong and Binh in November 1995 about the life of Red Dao people in Thanh Kim commune, Sa Pa district, intended to give a voice to Dao women at an international conference organised by the Institute of Ethnology about the future of the Dao people, to which women had not been invited.
- A film made by Binh to train Water Resources staff in participatory design techniques.
- A video made by Binh, Huong, and the former Country Representative to support the evaluation of a tree-nursery project based in schools.
- *Friend to Friend*, a children's video project run by Binh, in which young people talk to each other about their own lives, hopes, and fears.

In Laos, pilot-project participants from the agency CIDSE have trained other personnel in participatory video processes. In Indonesia, I.V. Domingo has set up a series of participatory video workshops for World Neighbors. She also ran a Communication for Development workshop organised by the NGO Training Project in Hanoi, at which the Oxfam Grassroots Video Team showed the tapes they had been working on.

Outcomes in the UK

Oxfam's Campaigns Unit decided to use the *Sea Dyke* tape made in Minh Duc and *Earth and Water*, the tape about the reservoir, for the 1996 round-Britain meetings of Oxfam supporters. The tapes were subtitled in the UK, using the same narrative structure as the originals, and transferred to professional-format Beta tape. On the question of copyright, debate has only just begun about a community's rights over its own media productions. As things stand, therefore, the notional of copyright in relation to the Ky Nam tapes must be seen as a moral rather than legal issue. However, permission to use the tapes for fund-raising and educational purposes was sought from the villagers and granted at this time.

Oxfam's Internal Communications team reported:

> ❧ The two Vietnamese videos are being used by Oxfam throughout the UK and Ireland as a catalyst input into local supporters' forums. The videos are shown to small groups of supporters from Oxfam's trading or campaign network, who then use the content for small-group work.
>
> Evaluations have shown that our supporters have been very impressed by the fact that the videos have been produced, filmed, and edited by staff, partners, and communities in the country, rather than by a film crew brought in from outside. They appreciate the direct and simple styles of the films.
>
> Some serious work needs to be done on the future use of this medium in the context of UK and Ireland supporter education and development. For example, would it be possible to set up processes that would allow our supporters to feed back directly to the video makers? ❧

These comments from the Campaigns Unit appear to reinforce the issue raised by the Ky Nam evaluation about the responsibilities created by the introduction of representational processes. The Oxfam supporters recognised that they had been addressed by the villagers of Ky Nam in these two tapes, and they felt that they should reply.

A half-day workshop was held in the Oxford head office of Oxfam by the Cross-Programme Learning Unit in December 1995, and attended by Desk Officers from the International Division and Campaigns and Communications personnel from the Marketing Division.

Lessons learned — and the way forward   7

The previous chapter evaluated the pilot project in Ky Nam in terms of the objectives defined in the original project proposal. This final chapter will examine the broader issues that arise from a consideration of the participation, representation, and re-presentation that took place in Ky Nam, viewed from the wider perspectives of training and learning in the field; it will also examine the institutional implications.

Personal bias and other narratives

In the three-day preparatory training, prior to the field-work stage of the pilot project, trainees used their own narratives as practice material for video recordings. They described their own social and cultural backgrounds to each other, and this expression of their personal identities opened the way for discussions of personal preferences and biases when the teams worked in the field. The introduction of personal narratives was intended also to raise awareness of cultural differences and divergent points of view, and to enable the team to use this consciousness in their approaches with village participants. Ground rules for team behaviour, and for the work with villagers, were established. The team established an ethos of openness, which was later reinforced in the daily sharing of experience in the field.

This process of recording and reviewing their own narratives as part of the preparatory training for field-work was seen as offering an experience which would be repeated with villagers in Ky Nam. Video recordings offer an opportunity for reflection on self-identity and group-identity which often proves valuable in enabling individuals and groups to gain confidence and to see themselves more clearly in relation to others. For example, when a woman in a village in Malawi saw herself for the first time on screen, reviewing and explaining a village map which she and other women had just drawn on the ground, she said: *'I know that it is me. But is it really me? Am I really an individual?'*

Values of reflective teaching and learning

We have seen that facilitation of field-work training operates at the level of training/teaching the trainees, and at the level of the interface between trainees and local people. At both levels, the aims are to enable the groups to develop analytical skills and to function critically and independently. The trainer guides the trainees, but enables the trainees to appropriate the direct relationship which is established with local people, and the greater knowledge they gain about the local groups and contexts. In turn, the trainees facilitate the local groups, but enable them to appropriate the knowledge gained about their own lives through the process.

Sensitivity to contextual and cultural differences is important at each point on the continuum which begins with the training of facilitators, continues in the facilitation of local groups, and may end in relationships with local authorities and others beyond the village. The experiences of learning that facilitators gain during their own training will be reflected in their recognition of and response to culture and contexts.

Through their shared analysis of their own cultural contexts and differences in the preliminary workshop, trainees begin to gain awareness of the need to contextualise their approaches within the wider implications of local conditions: the economy, markets, local and national history and government, cultural and religious practices.

Rapport

Similarly, the values of rapport-building should be established both theoretically and practically within the preparatory workshop. 'Rapport' has been used in this case-study to describe a climate in which people work together with mutual respect and trust. Good rapport is, as Chambers says, a 'capability' that depends on 'personality',[1] but it also involves value judgements and trust. Trust determines how rapport is established within the workshop between trainees and trainer, as well as in the field between trainee facilitators and local people. Rapport in the workshop depends upon a positive assessment of the possibility that an exchange of teaching and learning can take place.

An understanding of the ways in which knowledge is produced in informal contexts should inform the expectations and activities of outsiders when they intervene in the lives of under-represented groups.

This case-study has emphasised the connection between participatory learning, the collective production of knowledge, and the re-presentation of learning in an active process of addressing audiences and authorities beyond the community. The value of this process lies specifically in the interactive learning between outsider/intervening facilitators, the authorities which govern the lives of those on the margins of society, and groups of poor people themselves. The potential of these learning processes was documented in the uses made of the Education tapes in Vietnam.

The experiential learning of NGO field-staff in this case-study indicates the value of field-work, even for experienced personnel. Participatory observation proved novel and valuable. Field-staff are usually task-driven, so the experience of just spending unstructured time with villagers, observing, participating in their lives, and losing their status as experts, is important and useful in enabling them to experience and re-assess villagers' capabilities. At the same time, a period of this kind of rapport-building enables the villagers to assess whether they wish to work with the outsiders.

The outsider team, especially when its composition is multi-national, and representative of several different organisations, constitutes another cultural context. It is important for the team members to deconstruct this context and to understand the biases and agendas which it represents before embarking on work in the field.

Transparency

The case-study has emphasised that an essential determinant of relationships between outsiders and insiders in the field is the perception which the local community forms of the identity of the facilitator(s). In the local context this judgement may be influenced by considerations of material benefits to be gained through the relationship; these expectations will, in turn, affect judgements about the value of the exchange of information and knowledge. Specifically, the expectation of material reward for participation in research, even where such rewards have not been discussed, influences the power-relations between the facilitators (representing their agencies) and the groups with whom they work. It can also influence the selection of agendas for research by local groups.

This case-study has been concerned with what was intended to be open-agenda field research. In the field-work context, these values should be established during the rapport-building phase (Phase 2). This phase determines how knowledge about the personal and organisational identity of the facilitator is communicated to local groups.

Participant observation enables outsiders and insiders to meet in the initial stages of field-work, to inform themselves about each other. However, this process requires careful preparation. Outsiders need to clarify their personal and organisational motives for engaging in field-work and be prepared to communicate these motives clearly to local people.

Monitoring transparency is central to all stages of the process of producing and representing knowledge. In other words, the relationships which inform representations of information should be apparent and accessible both to the sender and the receiver. The identity of the interveners is always of great concern to local groups, and clarity about identity and intention demands sensitivity and honest analysis on the part of the interveners at the preparatory stage. All the possible implications of the villagers' often unspoken question — *'What are you doing here?'* — need to be understood. Reflection on this question should form part of the formulation of any project, and for field-workers it will need personal as well as operational answers, which will inform the transparency with which they can represent their interests and their roles to local people.

Responsible risk-taking

Another aspect of transparency is the relationship between development professionals and other players. This is particularly sensitive in work involving participatory learning, representation, and the recorded media. Is the project team able to answer the question *'What are you doing here?'* in the same way to all the players? The same answer for all may be the ideal, but if variations appear to be politically necessary, then indicators of risk emerge, and it will be important to consider who is at risk. It is possible that the consequences of risk will ultimately be borne by the local groups, and this indicates the need to examine whether the project should be modified in a way that would allow the same answer to be given to all parties.

Decisions about risk-taking should not be made on behalf of the local participants. As we have seen from this case-study, in relation to the parents' decision to risk speaking in public about the corruption in the primary school, once participants decide their own agendas for participatory research, they can then decide how and whether they wish to represent the knowledge that emerges, in what they perceive to be the appropriate public sphere.

One implication of placing the choice of the public sphere for re-presentation in the hands of local people is that omitting to do so, as we saw in case of negotiations with funders for the Ky Nam sea dyke, also signifies a lack of transparency about who holds the power over the knowledge that villagers have produced.

Principal findings

Learning activities recorded and retrieved on video in the original language and context can be reviewed and given a more structured significance by the participants, through the selection of sequences. For example, after viewing the tape of their own discussion and the debates about the models they made of their villages, the village editorial teams were able to suggest songs and views of the village which would give further background and depth to their representations.

The questions that have to be addressed throughout these processes are *who does what, when, and why?* The answers lie in the appropriation of the ownership of knowledge and representation by local people. The process of video recording must be made accessible to the participants, so that they can direct the camera and use it as their note book. At these initial stages in the uses and development of participatory media, the most pressing issue is to ensure equality of representation, rather than training one or two members of a community to become technical experts. The participants must be allowed to take over the role that in traditional film-making would be accorded to the director. It is important to introduce the camera to everyone, and to demystify its operation, but not necessarily at this stage to train villagers to act as camera operators. The process by which villagers take over the direction of the camera evolves through a number of stages, as we saw from the case-study. In the early research stages, it is necessary for the facilitating team to demonstrate not only the camera, but how meaning can be sequenced. This is the process referred to by Herman Mondaca when he described the role of his team: 'to receive views and return them to the people in a structured way'.[2]

We saw in Ky Nam that the process of regular review of the tapes with the participants must offer them the opportunity, even at the early stages, of critically considering how their meaning has been represented. The way is then opened to the participants later in the process to take over direction of their tape, and for even the least-represented in the group — in this case the women — to ask for changes or additions — as they did in Minh Quy, when asking for sequences to be added about income-generation. The role of the facilitator of participatory video is to ensure that everyone has access to the recording process. The training of individuals in camera work and editing, in the initial stages of using participatory video with a local group, presents the possibility of excluding the weakest members by empowering the already powerful. The danger that might arise from this is illustrated by the difficulty experienced by even the Vietnamese members of the pilot-project team in distinguishing politically appointed 'participants' from others in Ky Nam. The technical aspects of small camcorders are easier to assimilate than issues of critical consciousness and representation, and technical training can be offered later in the process.

The findings of this case-study show that the making of meaning using this participatory approach to video passes through several stages. The camera is introduced and demonstrated, and the images it produces are discussed with the participants. The use of the camera to record sequences of learning and to play them back to the participants is demonstrated. The meaning of this learning is reviewed and discussed. Finally, the participants take over the direction of the camera to record sequences and statements to represent knowledge arising from the learning sequences. The facilitators of the recording process consistently reduce their input to the structure of meaning. The aim is not necessarily to create local video-makers, but rather to enable local people to inscribe meaning and to practise representation and re-presentation.

Interventions by development practitioners should be shaped by local forms of expression, and outsiders should be able to respond to these with sequences of learning activities using appropriate forms. Local people should not be required to learn and reproduce a series of universally applied participatory research methods.

The participatory use of video can record and reflect preferred languages and literacies (which might include dance, drama, songs, and poems). At the same time, it offers the means of focusing attention on issues selected by the participants, and the opportunity for retrieval and reflection of different views.

Using video in a participatory process raises local awareness of the alternative uses of the medium. It also creates opportunities for learning among other players beyond the participant local group. In Vietnam the comments made about all the tapes, by the officials from the District Education Department, as well as by the Chairman of Ky Anh District in Vietnam, show their consciousness of the different values of the people's representation, compared with the programmes made currently by their own broadcast station.

The perceived boundaries of communication

In the field it is important to understand the social and cultural boundaries of the State, the village authorities, and the family, and how these affect issues of power and authority. The structure of these boundaries will inevitably affect perceptions of what constitutes the public sphere in a specific context. In Vietnam, although the State is in a process of transition, the government and the family are still perceived as structurally united, and the public sphere is therefore generally perceived as equated with the interests and opinions of the government; whereas in the West the public sphere constitutes 'public opinion' (the general opinion of groups of private citizens). However, as we noted in Vietnam, this boundary is beginning to change.

The concept of 'preferred literacies' prioritises thinking about cultural contexts. It enables us to consider forms of recorded meaning, and it gives us the opportunity to compare these other forms of cultural expression with what

Oxfam/Ben Fawcett

above 'Only now, watching the video, we realise how beautiful our place is.'

is often seen as the literacy of outsiders and their organisations. The dangers of transforming local forms or codes of expression at source are clearly related to issues of access to representation and communication. [3]

The focusing property of the camera can have a similar function to the focusing tools used in traditional PRA. At the same time, the distancing function of the recorded image gives meaning a new significance, without transforming the code. This was demonstrated when the villagers spoke of suddenly recognising the beauty of their own environment. And the villagers' own poetry and songs gave a greater depth of meaning to the cultural values they place on their environment.

Participation and representation in development processes

This account of a training workshop in participatory video techniques has raised the issue of where participation begins and ends. We have seen that local people can benefit from practising representation, and that they can use the research to analyse local conditions and options.

However, the case-study has raised as many questions as answers about how participation in the construction of representation is addressed by the players in development beyond the local context: by NGOs, government bureaucracies, and donors. Participation is a multi-dimensional undertaking in any development context. As Schon[4] points out, the reality which faces all practitioners in the field can be compared to a marsh, and in the marsh lie the problems of greatest human concern. Mosse[5] raises a crucial consideration when he asks whether the concept of intensive field-work practice and learning, implied by the notion of participation, can be achieved in the contemporary climate. He is referring to the problem of the human and financial resources required for the promotion of intensive, locally based approaches, and the effects of the shifts towards local resource-management and cost-recovery which have been influenced by both international donors and domestic policy.

Participatory planning is now part of the orthodoxy of poorly equipped public-sector systems. For example, in Ky Nam we witnessed how the 'new participatory orthodoxy' had been included in a nominal way in a government-to-government loan programme in Ky Nam. The Commune People's Committee had been made responsible for disbursing German government loans, made available through the Vietnam government's poverty-alleviation programme; but the CPC in Ky Nam had been offered no training, and there is no training for local people who accept loans under the scheme. As a result, poor families receiving relatively large, low-interest loans may spend the money wastefully: one example in Minh Quy was the purchase of cows for income-generation by farmers who had no experience and no fodder; the cows subsequently died. Not only will there be no recovery of the loan, but there will be no economic recovery for the farmer either.

We may continue to debate how political and cultural relationships affect participation. But this case-study has shown that we must be concerned with sustainable processes. The right to representation is at the root of participation, but these processes often mark a significant departure from existing bureaucratic systems and procedures, and they may appear to offer little gain to those who are asked to implement them in the field. The new accountability may even be seen to represent a loss.

NGO staff create a cultural climate for development which affects the attitudes of local government bureaucrats, who often envy their mobility and their *per diem* payments. Ultimately this NGO culture is, in turn, affected by the places in which NGOs site their offices — often in capital cities — and by the location of their various programme areas, as well as by the agreements they have made with donors and national governments. These are the conditions that determine the boundaries that are seen as acceptable for the 'new participatory orthodoxy'. It is a climate in which participation by local people in a continuum of representation and response, extending beyond the village or local sphere, is difficult to incorporate into the annual budgets and strategic plans of international NGOs, government bureaucracies, or donors. Nevertheless, the management of such budgets, their sources and their disbursement should be characterised by a development strategy of transparency, which enables all the parties to understand and evaluate needs, resources, and beneficiaries.

In the present climate I could be accused of presenting a utopian proposition. It has not been my purpose to examine how to change NGO or local-government management, but rather to challenge the limitations of the boundaries of the 'new orthodoxy'. I have wanted to show, through the relationship of informal and formal learning, why changes should be made if participatory development aims to create an independent and critical society. The ways in which funding is made available are part and parcel of a pedagogical experience about survival that should not be concealed, but rather should become a transparent process. The implications of such transparency may well be that there should be a greater priority given to project workers living alongside local people. This was indicated by the experience in Ky Nam, where it was clear that the short field visits that could be afforded by Oxfam's programme officers in the course of a normal year, travelling from Hanoi, did not give them access to the insights and knowledge of local people and groupings which would have made it possible to monitor the status of the participants in the video pilot project. This implies that such brief visits would not suffice either to develop the representation of local groups in their dealings with government bureaucracies.

While the focus of this case-study has been on the participatory training and uses of video, several of the principal findings have been about development practice and its management. These findings have confirmed the need to re-examine the purpose of development, and to clarify the role of participatory learning and its implications for representation by local people.

There is a clear link between the training of the development practitioner and the processes that he or she will use to encourage local groups and the related players to communicate with each other in responsive ways. Yet there is a danger that the traditional academic separation between theory and practice will be reproduced within the management of the development processes under the auspices of the modern development NGO. The risk is that practical processes of local participatory learning become separated from the processes of representation. So while local groups may practise participatory learning, NGO staff will undertake the representation of local group learning in the public sphere. The problem with this dislocation is that a vital aspect of critical learning for the local groups is excluded or omitted. When the new knowledge gained through participatory learning is re-presented by others, outside the context in which it was acquired, it becomes invisible to the local groups who generated the learning in the first place. This was the important lesson to be drawn from the villagers' sense of ownership of the education tapes, compared with the other two tapes about the sea dyke and about water-storage and irrigation in Ky Nam.

The model?

Case-studies of participatory processes can produce learning about learning, but should not be seen as methods to be reproduced irrespective of context. The case-study is created by its context, and learning should be critically reviewed throughout the process. Case-studies may result in success and failure on a variety of time-scales and on a variety of levels, but they cannot be accorded the status of a methodology.

The public sphere of the mass media has marginalised many of the world's poor, who are represented as hopeless and helpless, with problems that bear little relation to the values and representations of the mainstream. Development practitioners, academics, and activists have discussed ways in which the poor can be enabled to break the silence and to enter into dialogue with the wider world. However, as Mosse points out, even the participatory processes, such as PRA, employed by many NGOs in project planning are 'not matched in the structures and practices of implementation'.[6] The questions asked about participation in a local public PRA/PLA are not asked of other players within the implementing NGOs, local and national governments, or donor organisations. Mosse describes this gap in the participatory process: '... PRA reports sit on office shelves, and charts and maps provide attractive wall decoration and public statements about participatory intentions. The PRA ... provides a licence which permits any subsequent activity and decision-making to be labelled "participatory".'

This case-study has addressed the issue of the marginalisation of people's participation in representing their concerns and needs, and their knowledge about the causes of their poverty. The parts played by geo-political and economic contexts, by culture, and by the identity of those who intervene in the development of local groups have been seen to determine how poor people gain access to representation, and to influence how they perceive the appropriate sphere for public negotiation. There are, nevertheless, some specific theories which arose from this study. These are discussed in the next sections.

The transformation of the (relative) public sphere

We have learned from this study that, compared with the public sphere of the mass media, for groups at the margins of society the public sphere may be relatively private. In these contexts, I have referred to family groups in relation to the Party or Commune Committee in the same village. The transformation of this semi-public/semi-private sphere occurs when the excluded members of society share common interests, and are strengthened by this realisation to re-present themselves in a wider forum (in this instance, to the District and the Education authorities). As a result, a semi-public sphere is transformed, and may also become transforming in relation to the larger public sphere beyond, including the mass media. However, it is necessary for practitioners to attempt to understand local perceptions of these boundaries in terms of each context for work with participatory representation.

When assumptions are made on behalf of local groups about the boundaries of local perceptions of the public sphere, this can lead to risk-taking for which local participants may not be prepared. Such boundaries are clearly not permanent; as representation increases, notions about the extent of the relevant public sphere will change. If the boundaries are misjudged, local groups may be excluded from representation in public arenas which they understand are relevant, as in the case of Ky Nam villagers who in relation to funding perceived the relevant public sphere as both national and international. There is, then, a potential relationship in the practising of representation between relatively private and appropriate public spheres, and the transformation of representation within the truly public sphere or within the mass media.

Identity

When people learn together in informal groups, they may become more aware of themselves in relation to others — a process which can have an energising effect on the participants. It may also lead to conflict with the individuals or groups who are defined by the learners as 'others'; but there is also the possibility that both sides (in the case of Ky Nam the under-represented villagers and the authorities) will re-assess the identities they have imposed on the other.

When learners recognise that they have choices, they begin to develop what Freire has called 'critical consciousness',[7] which breaks through the passivity engendered by seeing the present merely as an acquisition from the past. Naming the other camp leads to the possibility of humanising it. We can see in the remarks of the District Chairman of Ky Anh, expressing his surprise at the villagers' demonstration of their capabilities, that this process of humanisation can have a two-way effect. The 'other' — in this case the villagers — by making statements about themselves have also humanised themselves in the eyes of authority. In this sense we can say that the construction of meaning and the representation of meaning is a process of developing critical consciousness about oneself and the outside world.

Renewable representation

The processes of representation and re-presentation through participatory video are not static and must be constantly renewed. In the early stages, the role of the facilitator is necessary to encourage the involvement of all the players. Response and dialogue need to be encouraged by development practitioners in the fora of the semi-private and appropriate public spheres.

Participatory video: concluding remarks

In this case-study I have been concerned to ask whether the domination of mass-media culture over the forms of television production may have conspired to cause us to ignore the alternative developmental uses of the technology. The focus has been on approaches to training for reflective practice, and using the technological possibilities of video in contexts where people are marginalised by the dominant media, to enable them to research and represent their own strategies for survival.

Governments of under-represented people often see participatory development as a marginal, time-consuming, and possibly dangerous activity. Infrastructural or industrial investment, involving inter-governmental negotiations about power and control, and the consequent determining of world pecking-orders, supports a rationale for the oppression of critical voices among the poorer populations. Yet, in what must often seem a paradoxical demand, international donors are insisting more and more on 'local participation' as a criterion for their aid.

Development agencies have pioneered the thinking about the dangers of creating aid-dependency. However, their own internal management structures, as well as their dependency on the funding of international donors, have often masked the connection between capacity-building for critical awareness with poor people, and the issues surrounding the representation by poor people of their own concerns, in the wider public sphere. Development agencies are confronted by the dilemma of process versus funding, and the problem of meeting developing-country governments' expectations of funds.

The ability to evaluate communication critically at the level of daily life is particularly important for under-represented people, in contexts where communication as exchange and representation, even at the local level, between women and men, caste or political groups, may have been restricted.

For poor people, critical awareness and communication/ representation are further complicated by power structures, oppressive, benevolent, or patriarchal, which also operate at national level between governments, and between government and people. At issue is the degree to which governments will tolerate representation from within civil society, as well as the degree to which individual governments see themselves as able to respond. International debt and structural adjustment play their part in formulating and reinforcing the attitudes of governments, and their reluctance to listen to the less powerful voices within civil society. The 'new participatory orthodoxy' is being imposed in a period when the philosophies of modernisation still form the *sine qua non* of the thinking and economic strategies of the governments of poor people.

The findings of this case-study may be seen as indicating the need for close daily contact between field-workers and local people. Aid funding is seldom transparent, at either the international or the local level, and money passes through many layers of beneficiaries before it reaches the poor.

Transparency is always an issue at the local level, and the validity of communication in the eyes of individuals is determined by popular conceptions of the interests influencing the news-givers. A central concern of those involved with progression in community development must be this relationship between communication, power, and representation — between the micro and the macro worlds at all levels; within village populations, and between different social strata within communities; between local communities and local government; and between local, national, and international governments; as well as between government and the voluntary sector.[8]

Video is not the only medium available through which local people can make themselves heard beyond their immediate context, and with which they can record and retrieve the responses of authority. It is, however, the only medium to date that records both image and sound, and makes it instantly retrievable. The participatory uses of video offer opportunities for representation and dialogue through which excluded people can be heard in the public and semi-public spheres from which they have been marginalised.

The question of training and facilitation has been emphasised in this case-study, because the introduction and sustainable management of a cycle of participatory research, representation, and response indicates the need for a new kind of reflective field-worker — living and working alongside under-represented communities — critically conscious of the economic, cultural, and social contexts of the local groups and their relationships with other players.

After word

In this case-study I have tried to give a narrative account of participatory video pilot project in Ky Nam, and then to view it from as many perspectives as possible. I am sure that representation of some of these perspectives bears the marks of my own cultural bias, for which I apologise. In the end, though, the most important aspect of the pilot project to my mind has been that it has raised the issue of people's representation, both within Vietnam and within the participating organisations, CIDSE, Oxfam UK and Ireland, and World Neighbors; and last but not least with Oxfam supporters in the UK and Ireland. Although the pilot project took the limited form of a short training workshop, I hope that the lessons which have arisen will take us forward to a better understanding of the transforming potential of the medium of video.

Notes

Introduction

1 'Proposal for a Pilot Project on the Potential of Video as a Development Learning and Campaign Tool: Pilot Project for Ky Anh District, Vietnam', Oxfam UK and Ireland, Hanoi Office, internal document, 1995.
2 Nguygen Thanh Binh: 'Mangrove Forestation in Ky Anh District', Oxfam UK and Ireland, internal report.
3 S.J. O'Brien: 'East Asia: where the spectrum is dark', in Soley and Nichols (eds): *Clandestine Radio Broadcasting*, New York: Praeger, 1987.
4 Laurel Kennedy: 'Vietnam seeks political stability and economic growth' in *Media Development* 1/1995.
5 M. Heibert: 'Watch this space', *Far Eastern Economic Review*, 31 March 1994.
6 Ibid.

Chapter 1

1 Paulo Freire: *Pedagogy of the Oppressed*, Herder and Herder, 1970.
2 Robert Chambers: *Rapid Rural Appraisal: Rationale and Repertoire*, IDS Discussion Paper, University of Sussex, 1981.
3 Robert Chambers: *Rural Appraisal: Rapid, Relaxed and Participatory*, IDS Discussion Paper, University of Sussex, 1992.
4 David Mosse: *'People's Knowledge' in Project Planning: The Limits and Social Conditions of Participation in Planning Agricultural Development*, Overseas Development Institute, Network Paper 58, London 1995.
5 Robert Chambers in I. Scoones and J. Thompson (eds): *Beyond Farmer First* (London: Intermediate Technology Publications, 1994).
6 I. Christoplos: *Representation, Poverty and PRA in the Mekong Delta*, Research Report No. 6 from EPOS (Environmental Policy and Society), Linkoping University, 1996; L. van Broekhoven: *Participation: Issue or Non-Issue: Country Participatory Approaches Analysis — Vietnam* (prepared for SNV, Netherlands Socioeconomic and Technical Development Cooperation Organisation), 1996.
7 R. Melkote: *Communication for Development in the Third World, Theory and Practice*, Sage, 1991.

8 M. Tehranian: 'Where is the New World Order: At the End of History or Clash of Civilisations', paper presented at the Sixth MacBride Roundtable, 20–23 January 1994.

9 A. and M. Matterlart and X. Delcourt: *International Image Markets* (translated by D. Buxton), Comedia Publishing, 1984.

10 M. Tehranian: 'Communication and development' in D. Crowley and D. Mitchell (eds): *Communication Theory Today*, Polity Press, 1994.

11 Tape produced by students on the University of Southampton MA course, Television for Development, with Sudanese refugees in Uganda: *I Am the Mother and the Father of the Children* (1995).

12 I. Christoplos *op. cit.*

13 J. Habermas: *The Structural Transformation of the Public Sphere: An Inquiry into a Category of Bourgeois Society* (translated by T. Burger and F. Lawrence), Cambridge, Massachusetts: MIT Press, 1989.

Chapter 2

1 11,000 dong = US$1 in 1995.

Chapter 3

1 Jules Pretty: 'Participatory learning for sustainable agriculture', *World Development* 23: 210.

Chapter 4

1 R. Chambers (1992), op. cit.

2 Ibid.

3 Ibid.

Chapter 5

1 The budget for the project included £5,000 for editing and sub-titling the tapes in the UK, and £3,580 for equipment, including two cameras and four microphones for the Hanoi office.

Chapter 6

1 R. Riddell: *Judging Success. Evaluating NGO Approaches to Alleviating Poverty in Developing Countries*, ODI Working Paper No. 37 (London: ODI, 1990).

Chapter 7

1 R. Chambers (1992), op. cit.
2 H. Mondaca: 'Asi aprendemos' in D. Archer and P. Costello: *Literacy and Power* (London: Earthscan, 1990).
3 E. Michaels and F.J. Kelly: 'The social organisation of an Aboriginal video workplace', *Australian Aboriginal Studies* 1 (1984).
4 D. Schon: *Educating the Reflective Practitioner: Toward a New Design for Teaching and Learning in the Professions*, The Jossey-Bass Higher Education Series (1987).
5 D. Mosse, op. cit.
6 D. Mosse, op. cit.
7 C. Lankshear, 'Functional literacy from a Freirean point of view', in P. McLaren and P. Leonard: *Paulo Freire: A Critical Encounter* (London: Routledge, 1993).
8 N. Uphoff: *Local Institutions and Participation for Sustainable Development*, IIED Gatekeeper series no. 31, London: IIED.

Sources and further reading

van Broekhoven, L. (1996) *Participation: Issue or Non-issue: Country Participatory Approaches Analysis — Vietnam* (prepared for SNV, Netherlands Socioeconomic and Technical Development Cooperation Organisation)

Chambers, R. (1981) 'Rapid Rural Appraisal: rationale and repertoire' in *IDS Discussion Paper No 155*, Sussex: Institute of Development Studies

Chambers, R. (1992) *Rural Appraisal: Rapid, Relaxed and Participatory*, Discussion Paper 311, Sussex: Institute of Development Studies

Christoplos, I. *Representation, Poverty and PRA in the Mekong Delta*, Research Report No. 6 from EPOS Environmental Policy and Society, Linkoping University

Edwards, M. (1995) 'Getting the wisdom: educating the reflective practitioner' in Nabeel Hamdi (ed): *Education for Real*, London: IT Publications

Freire P. (1970) *Pedagogy of the Oppressed*, Herder and Herder

Freire, P. (1989) *Politics of Education*, Macmillan

Habermas, J. (1989) *The Structural Transformation of the Public Sphere: An Inquiry into a Category of Bourgeois Society* (translated by T. Burger and F. Lawrence), Cambridge Ma: MIT Press

Harding, T. (1997) *The Video Activist's Handbook*, London: Pluto

Heibert M. (1994), 'Watch this space', *Far Eastern Economic Review*, 31 March

Illich, I., (1970) 'Planned poverty: the end result of technical assistance', in I. Illich (ed): *Celebrations of Awareness*, Harmondsworth: Penguin

Kennedy, Laurel (1995) 'Vietnam seeks political stability and economic growth' in *Media Development 1*

Lankshear, C. (1993) 'Functional literacy from a Freirean point of view' in P. McLaren and P. Leonard: *Paulo Freire: A Critical Encounter*, London: Routledge

Matterlart, A. and M. and X. Delcourt (1984) *International Image Markets* (trans. D. Buxton), Comedia Publishing

Melkote, R. (1991) *Communication for Development in the Third Word, Theory and Practice*, London: Sage

Michaels, E., and F. J. Kelly (1984) 'The social organisation of an Aboriginal video workplace' in *Australian Aboriginal Studies* no. 1

Mosse, D. (1995) *'People's Knowledge' in Project Planning: the Limits and Social Conditions of Participation in Planning Agricultural Development*, Overseas Development Institute, Network paper 58, London: ODI

Nguyen Thanh Binh 'Mangrove Forestation in Ky Anh District', Project Officer Report, Oxfam (UK and Ireland) Hanoi

O'Brien, S.J. (1987) 'East Asia: where the spectrum is dark' in Soley and Nichols, (eds): *Clandestine Radio Broadcasting*, New York: Praeger

Oxfam (UK and Ireland) (1995) 'Proposal for a Pilot Project on the Potential of Video as a Development Learning and Campaign Tool: Pilot Project for Ky Anh District, Vietnam'

Schon, D. (1987) *Educating the Reflective Practitioner: Toward a New Design for Teaching and Learning in the Professions*, The Jossey-Bass Higher Education Series

Shaw, J. and C. Robertson (1997) *Participatory Video: A Practical Guide to Using Video Creatively in Group Development*, London: Routledge

Tehranian, M. (1994) 'Communication and development' in D. Crowley and D. Mitchell: *Communication Theory Today*, London: Polity Press

Tehranian M. (1994) 'Where is the New World Order: At the End of History or Clash of Civilisations', paper presented at the 6th MacBride Roundtable 20–23 January 1994

Uphoff, N. (1992) *Local Institutions and Participation for Sustainable Development*, IIED Gatekeeper Series No 31, London: International Institute for Environment and Development

Wayne, M. (1997) *Theorising Video Practice*, London: Lawrence and Wishart

Oxfam Development Casebooks

other titles in the series include:

● disabled children in a society at war

A Casebook from Bosnia

Rachel Hastie

This Casebook analyses the lessons for working with disabled children learned from a radical and ambitious programme initiated by Oxfam UK and Ireland at the height of the war in Bosnia.

The book analyses issues such as working on long-term social development projects in an unstable society, and the impact of conflict on different groups of disabled people when disability itself becomes politicized.

0 85598 373 6

● empowering communities

A Casebook from West Sudan

Peter Strachan and Chris Peters

An account of the Kebkabiya project, which began as an attempt to improve food security in the wake of a major famine. Oxfam initially managed all the project activities, but now responsibility has been largely transferred to a community-based organisation.

The account of the increasing involvement of the community, and the creation of democratic structures for managing the project, provides valuable insights into the way in which a participative approach to development can result in empowerment for communities.

0 85598 358 2

United Kingdom and Ireland

Oxfam (UK and Ireland) publishes a wide range of books, manuals, and resource materials for specialist, academic, and general readers.

For a free catalogue, please write to:

Oxfam Publishing,
274 Banbury Road,
Oxford OX2 7DZ, UK;
telephone (0)1865 313922
e-mail publish@oxfam.org.uk

Oxfam publications are available from the following agents:

for Canada and the USA: Humanities Press International, 165 First Avenue, Atlantic Highlands, New Jersey NJ 07716-1289, USA; tel. (908) 872 1441; fax (908) 872 0717

for southern Africa: David Philip Publishers, PO Box 23408, Claremont, Cape Town 7735, South Africa; tel. (021) 64 4136; fax (021) 64 3358.